FOOD FOR THE SOUL

FOOD FOR THE SOUL

But he answered and said, It is written,
Man shall not live by bread alone, but by
every word that proceedeth out of the
mouth of God.

– Matthew 4:4 KJV

LUVERTA HOOD BOULWARE

XULON ELITE

Xulon Press Elite
555 Winderley Pl, Suite 225
Maitland, FL 32751
407.339.4217
www.xulonpress.com

Unless otherwise indicatedScripture quotations taken from the King James
Version (KJV)–*public domain.*

Paperback ISBN-13: 978-1-66289-415-2
eBook ISBN-13: 978-1-66289-416-9

Acknowledgments

First, I will reverence my Heavenly Father who has poured out His Spirit upon me. He has given me the opportunity to share His love and compassion by encouraging mankind throughout another inspirational book.

A thankful praise to Editor and book Coach, Dr. Larry Keefauver for your Godly knowledge.

A special thanks to my good friend and Personal Assistant, and Editor, Pamela Gail Richardson.

A special thanks to my family and friends for your love and support, and a heartfelt thanks to all my Spiritual Leaders for your prayers and encouragements.

A special thanks to my Team at Xulon Press Publishing, for your guidance and support throughout another incredible journey.

Endorsements

O! Taste and see that the Lord is Good! God's Word is sweeter than a honey-cone, and "Food for the Soul." This book is a must read, put it on your a-list and share!

As you journey through the pages of "Food for the Soul," you'll experience a full course spiritual meal that will satisfy your soul.

Come! Eat and drink of the living water until your cup overflows. It is the Lord that restores our soul for His name sake. It is written, man shall not live by bread alone, but by every word that proceeds from the mouth of God.[Mattthew 4:4NKJ]. Keep feasting on God's Word, it is the bread of life and food for your soul.

The author [Luverta, serves as a scribe that hears from the Holy Spirit, and like a pen of a ready writer, she writes.

Apostle, Dr. Olia Alexander
International Speaker - Author
Host-Visionary: Dr. Olia TV Show
TNG TV Networks"
Host-'F@TT" – Feasting @The Table

"FOOD FOR THE SOUL" is truly food for the soul. It will strengthen your mind, your spirit and strengthen you emotionally as you navigate through life. This devotional will challenge you, encourage you, and it gives you the tools to live a successful spiritual life.

Malcolm Williams-Pastor

I believe that "[i]n the beginning was the Word, [then the Word became flesh] and the Word was with God, and the Word was God". I believe we as Christians sometime forget that the very thing we are looking for [God's Word], we are looking with; God is within us, therefore the Word we are looking for is within us. Ms. Luverta's book is a reminder that we are God's temple and the spirit of God dwells within us.

Larry Golden, Financial Analyst; Realtor; Inventor

Table of Contents

Introduction

Spiritual Nourishment

Beloved, I wish above all things that thou may prosper and be in health even as thy soul prospereth. (3 John 1:2)

Food For the Soul is simply saying, when we reverence God wholeheartedly and take heed unto His Word our souls are nourished, refreshed, restored, and renewed in Christ. As we follow the examples of Christ, believing, receiving, confessing, and applying His Word, we are empowered, encouraged, inspired, impacted, enlightened, influenced, strengthened, and released to do great things for the kingdom of God. *Food For the Soul* is spiritual nourishment which helps the Body, Soul, and Spirit to flourish, grow, mature, develop, and evolve allowing us to become the best version of Christ we can be.

The purpose of *Food For the Soul* is to awaken the people of God who are sleep, stagnant, complacent, or lying dormant to arise out of their sleep and start living out their God given potentials. It's time for the people of God to arise and be obedient to the will of God and to speak the "Logos" written Word of God. We must be about our Father's business, witnessing and winning souls for Christ. Know before we can reach other's, all must be well with our own soul salvation.

However, we must be in right alignment and standing in the Word of God. We must consider His thoughts and ways and His instruction and direction to reach the masses. God delights in seeing His people walk in faith, righteousness, holiness, godliness, freedom, truth, healing, wealth, success, and victory.

It is written, man shall not live by bread alone, but by ever word that proceedeth out of the mouth of God. (Matthew 4:4)

Luverta H. Boulware, 54 yrs. old, resides in Lancaster, S C. I have two adult sons, Julius L. Hood, and Ja'Miara L. Boulware, one granddaughter, Journey Elise Boulware. My calling has been fostering, mentoring, and serving Children for over 29 years. I feel a shift and God has anointed my hands to write by His Spirit as I hear from Him. I Enjoy reading, writing, walking, traveling, and spending time with my granddaughter. I thank God for my roots that were planted 42 years at Mt. Tabor A.M.E. Zion Church in Lancaster, SC. My life has never been the same after joining in 2015 the Next Dimension Church in Lancaster, S C. I'm thankful and grateful for the five-fold ministry Leader's teaching and preaching the Word of God. I'm a Mother, Mentor, Sister, Aunt, Friend, Grandmother, Writer and Author of True Testimonies, Food For The Soul and more books on the way. But most of all I am a woman after God's own heart.

To gain the most from this devotional, I suggest you read, reflect on, and answer the interactive sections of each devotion. These can be used for your daily reading and time with God prior to beginning your day.

-1-

God First

Seek ye first the kingdom of God and his righteousness and all these things shall be added unto you. (Matthew 6:33)

Start each day putting God first. He is the Alpha and Omega. He is the beginning and the end. Do not substitute other things or activities before God. He must be first in all areas of our lives.

Ask the Lord, "What can I do today that will bring glory and honor to Your name?"

As you prioritize day-to-day with God as your focus, you can accomplish so much more with your life.

As you allow God to be first in your life daily, watch and see a stream of God's goodness and His mercies following you all the days of your life.

"Your priorities must be God first, God second, and God third until your life is continually face to face with God."
- Oswald Chambers

1. Get in a place where you can commune and fellowship with the Father.

2 Ask the Lord, "What can I do today that will bring glory and honor to Your name?"

Pray: *Father God, I desire to serve You with every part of my life today. Please direct my steps and help me to clearly see the opportunities You place before me to bring You honor as*

I go through my day. My heart's desire is to put You first in everything I do today. In Jesus' name I pray.

3. Make a list of the ways you can put God first in everything you do today.

4. Do whatever He directs you to do as you go through your day.

5. Record what you did and the results you experienced.

Thank God for all He helped you to accomplish today and for His goodness and mercy He has shown you.

-2-

The Word Is Needful

Heaven and earth shall pass away, but my words shall not pass away. (Matthew 24:35)

God has given us His Word to meditate on day and night. His Word is life long and life changing. Everything we need is found in His Word.

- If you need instructions on how to live righteously.
- If you need healing or deliverance.
- If you need salvation and forgiveness.
- If you need a breakthrough or a miracle.
- If you need more love, it is found in the Word of God.
- If you need strength.
- If you need joy or peace in your life.
- If you need help with your finances and you desire an increase and overflow, God has a Word for you.
- If you desire a closer walk with the Lord, study, absorb, and apply His Word and see what happens.

Allow the Word of God to take root in your heart and show you His plan to meet your need.

1. Begin by circling your need or needs from the list above.

2. Write out your most urgent need:

Additional Need:

3. Look up your specific need or needs and find a scripture from God's Word pertaining to your need. Write out the scripture on the lines under your need.

4. **Pray:** *Father God, please send me Your wisdom from above so I may clearly see how Your Word will guide me to fulfilling this need(s) as You would have it be accomplished.*

5. Describe how you are going to use this wisdom and message from God's Word to receive His solution to your need(s).

-3-

Who He Is

For Who is God, save the LORD? And who is a rock, save our God? God is my strength and power: and He maketh my way perfect. (2 Samuel 22:32-33)

God makes the difference. He is everything and all things to us.

God is...

- A Friend and a Father. (Isaiah 64:7, 1John 3:1)
- A Protector and Provider. (Psalm 3:3)
- Our Refuge from the storms of life. (Psalm 46:1-3)
- Our Shepherd who leads, guides, and orders our steps onto a better pathway. (Psalm 23:1-6)
- The Prince of Peace, when the enemy tries to bring, chaos and confusion. (Isaiah 9:6)
- Our Sustainer, and Keeper and He can fill any void in our lives. (Psalm 54:4)
- Our Redeemer. Jesus paid the ultimate price by shedding His precious blood for the sins of this world. (John 3:16)
- The Author and Finisher of our faith and knows our ending as well as our beginning. (Hebrews 12:2, Isaiah 46:9-11)
- Immanuel–God with us. (Isaiah 7:14, Matthew 1:23)
- The Way, The Truth, and The Life. (John 14:6)
- A Faithful and Just God. (1John 1:9)
- Omnipotent, All powerful. (Luke 1:37)

- Omniscient All Knowing, All-Wise and All-Seeing. (Matthew 6:26-30, 10:29-30)
- Omnipresent, present everywhere at the same time. (Psalm 139:1-2)

Pause and read and reflect on each of the scriptures listed above. Record what you discover and how it will help you on your life's journey. Memorize the scripture that impacted you the most.

- Isaiah 64:7

_____

_____

- 1John 3:1

_____

_____

- Psalm 3:3

_____

_____

- Psalm 46:1-3

_____

_____

- Psalm 23:1-6

_____

_____

- Isaiah 9:6

_____

_____

- Psalm 54:4

_____

_____

- John 3:16

_____

_____

- Hebrews 12:2

_____

_____

- Isaiah 46:9-11

_____

_____

- Isaiah 7:14

_____

_____

- Matthew 1:23

_____

_____

- John 14:6

_____

_____

- 1John 1:9

_____

_____

- Luke 1:37

_____

_____

- Matthew 6:26-30, 10:29-30

_____

_____

- Psalm 139:1-2

_____

_____

Pray: *Father God, I thank You for Who You are and for how You help and guide my life every day.*

-4-

Start Living

I am crucified with Christ: nevertheless, I live, yet not I, but Christ liveth in me, and the life which I now live in the flesh I live by the faith of the Son of God, who loved me, and gave Himself for me. (Galatians 2:20)

Put a smile on your face. God has been so good to you and life is good. You cannot allow anyone or anything to steal your joy. You have so much to be thankful for. Stop looking at or complaining about your situation. Give it to God!

Take a moment and make a list of all you should be thankful for. Now, thank your Heavenly Father for all He has done for you.

The grave could not hold JESUS down. You shouldn't allow any situation or circumstances to get you down and cause you to linger in self-pity.

Declare:

- ➤ The joy of the Lord is my strength.
- ➤ I am going to start rising in strength and power.
- ➤ I am going to start living my best life today!
- ➤ I know Christ died for me, so I am going to start living a faith-filled life.

Just breathe! Start living! Enjoy Life!

Pray: *Father God, I thank You that when people ask why I am always smiling, I can boldly tell them the joy of the Lord is my strength.*

-5-

Work the Word

Heaven and earth shall pass away, but My words shall not pass away. (Mathew 24:35)

Work the Word of God and the Word will work for you. In other words, take what God has said and apply His Word, principles, doctrine, teaching, and instructions to your life.

To apply His Word in your life, you need to...

> ➢ *activate His Word by faith*
> ➢ *apply the Word to your life*
> ➢ *believe the Word and speak it out loud*
> ➢ *receive the Word and thank God for His Word*
> ➢ *confess the Word over your life and watch His Word manifest in your life.*

The Word of God is alive and here for your usage. It is beneficial for spiritual development. His Word is at work in you even when you are not aware of it. Keep the faith. Remember the Word of God was here from the beginning of time, and it shall remain to the end of time.

Pray: *Father God, I thank You Your Word is always available and will meet my every need as I study, learn, and grow in wisdom and truth.*

-6-

Rich For a Purpose

It is easier for a camel to go through the eye of a needle, than for a rich man to enter into the Kingdom of God. (Mark 10:25)

Most people have a desire to become rich. As believers, we should want to be rich for a purpose other than to see how much material goods we can attain.

Our hope is in God, who richly provides us with everything for our enjoyment. Let us be about our Father's business by taking care of the poor and needy. Have a generous heart and give to charities and organizations that helps others live a happier and easier life.

We want to be rich with the purpose to advance the Kingdom of God and have the resources to complete the assignments God has place in our hands.

What is the assignment God has given you?

_____

_____

What do you need to accomplish your assignment?

_____

_____

_____

_____

Be aware, sometimes God supplies what you need for your assignment other than with money.

Have you received material items from others who have offered to help you with your assignment?

How can you use what God has blessed you with to bless others?

How are you using your talents to further the Kingdom of God?

Pray: *Father God, please give me wisdom from above and the strength to complete the assignment You have given me for today.*

-7-
Encourage Yourself

And David was greatly distressed; for the people spake of stoning him, because the soul of all the people was grieved, every man for his sons and his daughters: but David encouraged himself in the LORD his God. (1 Samuel 30:6)

When life happens, you can practice encouraging yourself. There may be times when your family and friends are not around, and you need strength and encouragement. This is when you must encourage yourself.

Encourage yourself by:

- ➤ Telling yourself you are strong and courageous.
- ➤ Declaring you will fight the good fight of faith.
- ➤ Reminding yourself you are more than a conqueror, an overcomer, and victorious.
- ➤ Remembering you are blessed of the Lord.
- ➤ You are His son or daughter.
- ➤ You are the righteousness of God.
- ➤ You are His representative.
- ➤ You are a friend of God.
- ➤ You are His workmanship; you are fearfully and wonderfully made.

Pray: *Father God, there are times I truly need to encourage myself. Please remind me of Your unfailing love and encourage me from Your Word to move forward on the path You have put before me.*

-8-

Giant Slayers

For the word of God is quick and powerful, sharper than any two-edged sword, piercing even to the dividing asunder of soul and spirit and of the joints and marrow as is a discerner of the thoughts and intents of the heart. (Hebrews 4:12)

God has equipped you with His most powerful weapon—His Sword which is His Word. When God's Word is abiding in you, you can operate under power and anointing. You can be a giant slayer! You can knock out or knock down any giants standing in your way of getting what God has waiting for you.

What is getting in the way of you receiving what God has for you?

The enemy may appear to be larger, stronger, and unbeatable. However, greater is He that is in you than he that is in the world. Your God is Mighty. He is unstoppable, unmovable, and unbeatable. The enemy is already defeated, and you are victorious.

Refuse to listen to the enemy's voice and his lies. Listen to the voice of the Lord calling you to be a giant slayer. You have heard the Lord saying, "Speak My Word, and the giants will fall." The Lord has given you dominion, power, and authority. He has anointed you to speak with confidence and boldness to slay giants.

Declare:

- Greater is he that is in me, than he that is in the world (1 John 4:4).
- God has given me victory through my Lord Jesus Christ (1 Corinthians 15:57).
- Jesus has given me dominion, power, and authority (Luke 10:19)
- Nothing can get in my way today; I am a giant slayer!

Pray: *Thank You Father, for standing with me through thick and thin and making me realize I am a giant slayer in the army of the Lord.*

-9-

Be Proactive

For as the body without the spirit is dead, so faith without works is dead also. (James 2:26)

Procrastinating is not being proactive or productive. This just means you keep postponing things. Being proactive is you controlling the situation and you knowing what will happen as you carry the plan of God out.

Here is your checklist:

- ☐ As a child of God, take charge and ownership of your responsibilities.
  What responsibility have you been postponing?

- ☐ Set realistic goals and hold yourself accountable.
  What goals do you need to complete God's plan for you today?

- ☐ Try to avoid anything that could interrupt you from living an effective and purposeful life.
  What have you allowed to interrupt you?

- ☐ Work towards your visions, goals, and dreams by being consistent and determine to do what is required of you.
  What are your visions, dreams, and goals for today and for your future?
  What is your first step toward fulfilling them?

- ☐ Try to surround yourself with those who have positive energy and passion to do great things.

Who is encouraging you to keep moving forward?
Who is holding you back?

Pray: *Father, my desire today is to serve and diligently keep moving forward and faithfully serve You by helping others in Your name.*

-10-

Praise In Advance

Let everything that hath breath praise the LORD.
Praise ye the LORD. (Psalm 150:6)

Always keep a praise on your lips, a praise of thanksgiving. Don't wait until trouble comes. Praise God in advance. Give the Lord praise through the good and bad.

Praise Him through your ups and downs.

Praise Him when you haven't seen the manifestations. Praise the Lord when you don't know how He will bring you out. What you do know is God is going to do it. Praise God in advance because you trust His Word over what the doctor's report says. Praise the Lord because you see, by the spirit, spiritual and financial doors opening. Send up a praise just because you love Him, and He is (Abba) Father.

Declare you will bless the Lord at all times, and His praise shall continually be in your mouth.

Start your day praising your Heavenly Father. The Psalms were written as songs. Choose one of your favorites and sing it as you begin your day.

Play praise music and sing along. Enjoy your drive or commute to work each day.

-11-

Chosen

*Ye have not chosen Me, but I have **chosen** you, and ordained you, that ye should go and bring forth fruit, and that your fruit should remain: that whatsoever ye shall ask of the Father in My name, He may give it you.* (John 15:16 emphasis added)

You were already chosen before the foundation of the world. Your life is already predestined by God. He has a plan and purpose for your life. You must agree with God and say, "Not my will Lord, but let Your will be done in me, through me, and for me." The Lord has **anointed** and **appointed** you to fulfill His purpose in the earth.

The Lord has **chosen** you to be His hands, feet, and voice to share the gospel with mankind, and to bring lost souls into His kingdom.

He has **chosen** you to encourage, inspire, impact, influence, strengthen, offer hope to the brokenhearted, and to lay hands on the sick so they can be healed.

It is an honor and a privilege to be chosen by God.

You were…

Chosen before _____

Chosen to be _____

    Why? _____

Chosen to also

Pray: *Thank You, Father, for anointing and appointing me to fulfill Your purpose in the earth. Not my will, Lord, but let Your will be done in me, through me, and for me, in Jesus' name.*

-12-

Suddenly

Suddenly there was a great earthquake, so that the foundations of the prison were shaken, and immediately all the doors were opened, and everyone's bands were loosed. (Acts 16:26 emphasis added)

God's timing is greater than our timing. There is no comparison. He is so amazing.

God can move suddenly, immediately, instantly, rapidly, miraculously, swiftly, and quickly.

My prayer is for any "doors" you need the Lord to open for you, are opened suddenly.

Ask Yourself...

What "prison doors" do I need God to open for me?

_____

_____

God's calling for your life will release you suddenly in His timing.

God is doing a new thing in the lives of His people, and He is performing it suddenly.

I declare, unto you by faith, by the time you get your prayer request out of your mouth, God has already answered and honored your prayers.

God will do it suddenly!

Record in your journal times when you have experienced God's "suddenlies" in your life.

_____

_____

_____

_____

Read these references to God's "suddenlies" in the Bible. Note how each one has helped you understand God's use of "suddenlies."

Numbers 12:4

2 Chronicles 29:36

Malachi 3:1

Luke 2:13

Acts 2:2

Acts 22:6

Pray: Heavenly *Father, I thank You for Your "suddenlies" in my life. I thank You for knowing what I need and when I need it.*

-13-

Fully Activate Your Faith

What doth it profit, my brethren, though a man say he hath faith, and not have works? Can faith save him? (James 2:14)

Put your faith to work. Allow your faith to operate in the things of God fully and completely. Allow your faith to operate for you.

Believe you shall receive everything God has for your life. Don't believe only a portion of God's goodness. Believe the full plan of God. Have the God kind of mountain-moving faith. Believe and trust God who is "faithful" in all His ways. Know your faith can cause things to shift in the spirit realm, as you continue to fully activate your faith.

There is nothing. God will withhold from His children.

He is waiting for you to speak those things that be not as though they were. Sometimes, you have not because you ask not. Believe, receive, and watch God work in your favor. When you fully activate your faith, be ready.

You are under an open Heaven.

Here is your "to do" list for activating your faith:

- o Believe you'll receive all God has for your life.
- o Have the mountain-moving kind of faith.
- o Believe and trust God who is faithful.

- Believe, receive, and watch God work in your favor.
- Remember, sometimes, you have not because you ask not.

Read these powerful scriptures to define, strengthen, and encourage your faith.

Hebrews 11:1 says faith is _____

_____

2 Corinthians 5:7 says we _____

_____

James 1:6 warns us to ask _____

_____

Hebrews 11:6 tells us it is impossible to _____

_____

Pray: *Thank You, Heavenly Father for teaching me in Your Word how my faith can cause things to shift in the spirit realm. Remind me, Father, to continue to fully activate my faith and faithfully serve You. Thank You for Your faithfulness.*

-14-

Something Happens

And this did she many days. But Paul being grieved, turned and said to the spirit, I command thee in the name of Jesus Christ to come out of her. And he came out the same hour. (Acts 16:18)

The works of the enemy are destroyed when you call on the name of JESUS!

You have the power and authority to **command** any unclean spirit which has you bound or held you captive, to release you now in the name of Jesus. Demons tremble at the name of Jesus.

There is wonderous working power in the precious blood of the Lamb. Sickness, pain, disease, lack, poverty, doubt, fear, wickedness, unforgiveness, and sin must leave when you call on the name of Jesus.

There is power, strength, victory, and breakthroughs taking place as you call on the name of Jesus.

Something happens when the children of God call on Jesus. There is power in His name!

JESUS! JESUS! JESUS!

Are you a child of God?
Are you exercising your power and authority?
Are powerful things happening in your life?

List the works of the enemy you need to destroy in your life. Call on the name of JESUS to destroy each one.

_____

_____

List what has you bound or held you captive. Command each one to release you in the name of Jesus.

_____

_____

Is there sickness, pain, disease, lack, poverty, doubt, fear, wickedness, unforgiveness, or sin in your life?

It must leave when you call on the name of Jesus.

Do you need a breakthrough today? What are you waiting for? Something will happen when you call on His name!

Pray: *Thank You, Jesus for the wonder-working power in Your name. Thank You no enemy can stand against You, no demon has power to resist You, and no obstacle can block Your plan and purpose in my life when I call upon Your name!*

Remember to record in your journal how you are experiencing the power in His name.

-15-

But God

But God, who is rich in mercy, for His great love wherewith He loved us, even when we were dead in sins, hath quicken us together with Christ (by grace ye are saved.) And hath raised us up together and made us sit together in heavenly places in Christ Jesus: That in the ages to come He might shew the exceeding riches of His grace in His kindness towards us through Christ Jesus. (Ephesians 2:4-7)

God can change your life. There are moments you know no one, BUT GOD could have done it.

- ➤ You didn't know how you or your loved one were going to come out of a situation, But God!
- ➤ You didn't know how long the sickness or disease was going to last, and then, you were completely healed. Another, But God!
- ➤ Your self-esteem was so low you didn't think you were important or mattered, then something happened to bring you encouragement, But God!
- ➤ You thought a loved one you had been praying for would never be set free from their addiction, But God!
- ➤ You thought your relationship or marriage was over, But God!
- ➤ You didn't think you could get a college degree at such a late age, But God!

Personalize these verses:

"But God, being rich in mercy, because of the great love with which he has loved _____ even when _____ was dead in _____ trespasses, made _____ alive together with Christ-by grace _____ have been saved." (Ephesians 2:4-5[1])

"_____ health may fail, and _____ spirit may grow weak, but God remains the strength of _____ heart...." (Psalm 73:26[2])

Describe a "But God" moment in your life:

_____

_____

_____

_____

Record this "But God" moment and watch for more of them as you go through your day. Record them in your journal and share them with others as a testimony of God's love.

Pray: *Father, I am so thankful for my "But God" moments. Thank You for always being there for me and with me. Thank You for the interventions You bring into my life just at the right time.*

---

[1] Taken from the ESV Bible Translation

[2] Taken from the NLT Bible Translation

-16-

Positioned

And whatsoever ye do, do it heartily, as to the Lord and not unto me: Knowing that of the Lord ye shall receive the reward of the inheritance: for ye serve the Lord Christ. (Colossians 3:23-24)

Are you in right standing with the Lord? Do you fear the Lord? If so, you are positioned for greater rewards. Positioning for greater rewards may require a shifting or a right alignment in your life to receive God's very best.

- ➤ Continue walking in love and obedience.
- ➤ Continue strengthening your brothers and sisters in Christ.
- ➤ Continue sharing the gospel of Jesus Christ.
- ➤ Continue winning souls for Christ's sake.

When you love on the poor and needy and show them kindness, you are positioned for greater blessings. When you minister to the men and women who are incarcerated, imprisoned, or confined, you are positioned for greater rewards.

Believe you are in the right position to receive the Lord's rewards, promises, and inheritance.

As you read these suggestions for ways to position yourself to serve the Lord, what other ideas came to mind?

_____

_____

_____

Positioning yourself for greater rewards may require a shifting or a realignment to receive God's very best in your life.

What areas may need realignment or shifting in your life to receive God's very best?

_____

_____

_____

_____

How are you going to accomplish these changes?

_____

_____

_____

_____

Pray: *Heavenly Father, please reveal to me any areas of my life where I need a shift or realignment. Then, please give me wisdom on how to make those changes Your way and in Your timing.*

In Jesus' name I pray.

Don't forget to update your journal concerning all you are learning about yourself and God's purpose in your life.

-17-

I'll Be the One

If any man serve Me, let him follow Me; and where I am, there shall also My servant be: if any man serve Me, him will My Father honour. (John 12:26)

Thoughtfully consider each of these questions inspired by this scripture. Do not answer too quickly because the Lord will take your answer as your word and expect your "Yea to be Yea."

Will you be the one who says, "Yes, God?"

Will you be the one who goes when no one else will go to serve and support the mission?

Will you be the one who will witness to others and lead them to Christ?

Will you be the one praying without ceasing?

Will you be the one interceding for others who may not be able to pray for themselves?

Will you be the one visiting the sick or feeding those who are hungry, thirsty, and lacking the necessities?

Will you be the one who goes behind the prison walls, speaking life and hope to those who will receive salvation and God's Word?

If this is you, say, "Lord, I'll be the ONE."

Sometimes, when we read a familiar scripture, we do not pause to reflect on what God is saying to us personally. Jesus' words in John 12:26 need to be taken very seriously. He is instructing and warning those who seek to be His true followers.

Jesus begins by saying, "If any man serve Me, let him follow Me."

What does this mean to you?

_____

_____

Then Jesus says, "and where I am, there shall also My servant be."

What does this mean to you?

_____

_____

Jesus closes by saying, "If any man serve Me, him will My Father honour."

How do you think God honors Jesus' true servants?

_____

_____

What does this mean to you if you do not choose to serve Jesus in the way He has instructed in this verse?

_____

_____

Don't forget to update your journal concerning what you have learned about yourself today.

-18-

No Separation

For I am persuaded that neither death nor life, nor angels nor principalities nor powers, nor things present nor things to come, nor height nor depth, nor any other creature, shall be able to separate us from the love of God, which is in Christ Jesus our Lord. (Romans 8:38-39)

Always give thanks unto the Lord for while you were yet a sinner. Christ died for you. Be determined or sold on the fact nothing shall come between you and God. Whether it be people, money, land, wealth, success, fame, material things, or sin. Remember, don't love things above God.

What this passage tells us, God will not pull away from us. If there is a separation, it is because we choose to pull away from Him. Don't allow anything in your life to cause you to choose to separate or pull away from God.

Read the parable of the prodigal son.

Why did the son choose to separate himself from his father?

What did the father do?

How did the father respond when the prodigal son chose to return to his father?

What did you learn from this parable about God your heavenly Father?

Acknowledge the Father, the Son, and the Holy Spirit, the Trinity. They are one and cannot be separated.

Read what Jesus prayed in John 17:21-23.

Who is Jesus praying to?

What was He praying to happen?

_____

_____

Who did He want this to happen to?

Pray: *Thank You, Lord, that while I was yet a sinner. You died for me. Thank You for Your promise in Romans 8:38-39 that nothing shall separate Your love from me. Please warn me if I begin to pull away from You. I do not want to allow anything to come between us.*

Don't forget to update your journal concerning all you are learning from God's Word.

-19-

It's Already Done

*When Jesus therefore had received the vinegar, He said, **It is finished**: and He bowed His head, and gave up the ghost.* (John 19:30 emphasis added)

Jesus knew what His mission was when He came to earth. He finished the work on the cross at Calvary.

Whatever you are asking God for, it's already done. When Jesus said, **"IT IS FINISHED,"** He was saying everything had been settled in heaven. The answers to any problems, questions, or concerns you have. It's found in His Word.

Believe by faith these things are already done through Jesus Christ, your Lord and Savior. Your healing, deliverance, breakthrough, financial increase, and favor are already done.

You are to fulfil your mission. Pray and believe others you know will live a blessed and God-fearing lifestyle as you walk in God's anointing.

Daily start your day by confidently declaring God's goodness over every area of your life because it's already done.

List any problems, questions, or concerns you are facing in your life.
Find the answer to each one in His Word.

_____

_____

_____

_____

Write it out and declare it daily until you see the final work.

_____

_____

_____

_____

_____

Record in your journal when the finished work is manifested in your life.

Pray: *Thank You, Lord Jesus for the finished work of the cross. Thank You for declaring this finished work so I can walk in my anointing and declare the finished work in my life as well in others' lives.*

-20-

Have Substance

Better is the poor that walketh in his uprightness, than he that is perverse in his ways, though he be rich. (Proverbs 28:6)

It's very important for God's sons and daughters to have good morals. Substance can be defined as having good morals.

Ask Yourself...

How do I define good morals?

_____

_____

Do I have good morals as a child of God?

When we are spiritually matured, we know right from wrong. Substance can also be defined as knowing right from wrong.

Whether a person is rich or poor, they both can display or demonstrate honesty, fairness, virtue, trust, decency, faith, patience, and wisdom.

Ask Yourself...

Do I demonstrate, honesty, fairness, virtue, trust, decency, faith, patience, and wisdom with my life?

Which ones do I need to work on?

The Lord is pleased to see His children walking in integrity. Substance can also be defined as walking in integrity.

These moral principles and seeking to walk in integrity can keep us grounded, humbled, and satisfied with what we have. It's great to have material goods, but it's greater to have substance.

Substance reflects the love of God, faith, hope, joy, peace, strength, gentleness, power, authority, dominion, meekness, self-control, patience, holiness, godliness, and righteousness.

Ask Yourself...

Does this describe me?

Pray: *Father God, I desire to please You with my life. Help me to continually seek to be a person of substance as defined by You in Your Word. Please show me where my weaknesses are and how I can improve myself today and every day.*

Don't forget to update your journal concerning all you are learning about yourself.

-21-

Obedience Brings The Blessings

But He said, Yea rather, blessed are they that hear the word of God, and keep it. (Luke 11:28)

Applying God's Word is imperative for our spiritual growth. We shouldn't hear the Word only, but do what His Word has commanded us to do. Walk in obedience and follow God's instructions and directions. Our Heavenly Father will bless His children abundantly. There are godly principles we must simply apply to see God's manifestations and His fullness.

Remain faithful, walk in love and obedience.

Read:

James 1:22-25 says we should not _____
Because if we do then we _____ ourselves.
Instead, we are to _____.

What does this passage say about the one who obeys?

_____

_____

*What does it say about the one who does **not** do what it says?*

_____

_____

What did Jesus explain to His followers in John 15:10 about obedience to God's commands?

_____

_____

Pray: *Father God, I truly want to see spiritual growth in my life. Please show me how to apply Your Word as I seek Your guidance each morning. Please forgive for those times I have not been obedient to Your Word.*

Remember to record in your journal how obedience to God's Word has brought God's blessings into your life.

-22-

My Life Echoes

But the fruit of the Spirit is love, joy, peace, long suffering, gentleness, goodness, faith. meekness, temperance, against such there is no law. (Galatians 5:22-23)

When strangers, unbelievers, or believers of the "Word of God" encounter you, what is your life saying to them? ____
_____

Can others discern you belong to God? _____

Are you a light which shines in the darkness? _____

Can they see Jesus in you? _____

Does your countenance say you are blessed and highly favored of the Lord? _____

When you speak, does love and joy ring out of you? _____

Can others you have encountered see you have a meek and humble spirit? _____

Can people tell you are a peace maker? _____

Do you have or practice self-control? _____

Will you hang in there, stay the course, demonstrate self-control and endurance? _____

Are you on the right path? _____

Every day let your life echo the "Fruit of the Spirit."

List the Fruit of the Spirit. Define each one. Indicate if your life echoes each of them.

_____

_____

_____

_____

_____

_____

_____

_____

Pray: *Father God, thank You for the Fruit of the Spirit. I truly desire to show others each one of them in my actions and my words. Please show me where I need improvement.*

Remember to record in your journal if you are on the right path as far as exemplifying the Fruit of the Spirit in your life.

-23-

Living Proof

For thou shalt be His witness unto all men of what thou hast seen and heard. (Acts 22:15)

You have not only seen and heard of the love of Jesus Christ, but you have accepted Jesus as your Lord and Savior. You have received salvation; and you are born again. You have developed a personal relationship with the Father and now you know Him. You are a witness of God's goodness, firsthand. You are living proof Jesus is real and alive because He lives inside of you.

Jesus is the reason we live, move, and have our being.

You are living proof God pours out His goodness on His people. You have witnessed the True and Living God speaking into your heart and showing His compassion.

Continue being a great example and witness of Jesus Christ. You are living proof of His righteousness.

Describe your salvation experience,

_____

_____

_____

_____

How did your life change after you developed a relationship with Jesus Christ?

_____

_____

_____

_____

In what ways has God poured out His goodness in your life?

_____

_____

_____

_____

Declare: Jesus is the reason I live, move, and have my being.

Pray: *Thank You, Heavenly Father for Your beloved Son, Jesus Christ and His love and compassion in my life. I know He is the reason I live, move, and have my being. I am living proof!*

-24-

Check Your Heart

Create in me a clean heart, O God, and renew a right spirit within me. (Psalm 51:10)

Ask Yourself...

Am I still holding a grudge against someone?

Why?

Have I forgiven the person who hurt or offended me?

Why not?

It is time for you to check your heart, forgive, and move on. Ask the Lord to guard your heart from day-to-day. You should even ask Him to give you; His heart. His heart loves and forgives at all times. The Bible tells us the pure in heart shall see God. We don't want anything to block or stop us from seeing our Heavenly Father one day face-to-face. People may look at your outward appearance, but the Lord looks at your heart.

Examine your heart and see what condition your heart is in.

Is my heart clean? _____

Do I have the heart of God? _____

How can I know? _____

Pray: *Father God, please give me Your heart. Help me to create a clean heart so others see Your love, compassion, and forgiveness through me.*

In Matthew 12:34, what did Jesus say about the connection of a heart with what we say?

_____

_____

_____

_____

Read, write out, and memorize Proverbs 23:7.

_____

_____

_____

_____

-25-

God's Word

Thy testimonies are wonderful: therefore, doth my soul keep them. The entrance of Thy words giveth light; it giveth understanding unto the simple. (Psalm 119:129-130)

The Word of God gives light, order, insight, favor, guidance, direction, instruction, wisdom, knowledge, and understanding. His Word also counsels, teaches, promises, and gives manifestations and revelations. We are to take heed to the truth given to us by God in His Word for this is our daily bread.

Each one of us will have our own testimonies about how we made it through this or that. If you haven't been tested, tried, or gone through the fire, the older Saints will say, "Just wait awhile." Or maybe you know of someone who has; and their testimony is: God is so wonderful! He is a merciful and gracious God.

Apply His Word to shed light in your life. The Lord has made His Word simple, plain, and beautiful for His people to grasp its true meaning for their lives.

You may have heard someone testify and say God has taken their test and made it their testimony after they have gone through a trial and come out the other side with God by their side.

Have you experienced a "test" in your life and come through it?

Did you realize God was by your side bringing you through it?

Take the time to thank Him and then write out how this test has now become your testimony and record it in your journal.

Pray: *Thank You, Father God for never leaving me even during the tests of my life. Show me how to share my testimony so I can give hope and encouragement to those who may be going through their own time of testing.*

My Testimony:

_____

_____

_____

_____

_____

_____

-26-

Be A Visionary

And it shall come to pass afterward, that I will pour out My Spirit upon all flesh; and your sons and your daughters shall prophesy, your old men shall dream dreams, your young men shall see visions. (Joel 2:28)

If you are a visionary, you take risks, and you think outside of the box.

You see what others don't see. Realize, God has given you this great gift.

What are you doing with the visions God has given you?

_____

_____

Dream big and challenge yourself to do what others say cannot be done.

Pay attention to your dreams. If a creative idea comes to your mind, pursue it.

How are you pursuing the creative ideas God has given you through your dreams?

_____

_____

_____

_____

The Lord has anointed you to do great things on earth. It's your responsibility to follow the vision or dream He has given to you.

God is showing you His unmerited favor.
Trust in the Lord, and He will do,
some amazing things in your life.

Have you been afraid to pursue the dreams or visions God has given you?

Ask Him to show you the first step of faith you need to take. When you trust Him, watch how He pours His favor out in your life. Record in your journal the amazing things He does in your life.

Pray: *Father, thank You for giving me dreams and visions. I now know it is my responsibility to pursue them, one step at a time. Please show me that first step. I look forward to the amazing things You are going to do in my life!*

-27-

Hurting People

He healeth the broken in heart, and bindeth up their wounds. (Psalm 147:3)

Hurting people sometimes hurt other people unknowingly. Sometimes the hurt or the wound is old and deep, and the pain has never been dealt with. If this is not you, you may know of someone in this type of situation. They have suppressed the hurt or pain on the inside. Later, it became anger, bitterness, resentment, and unforgiveness. Tell them to turn to the Lord. He is a Healer.

God will remove any forms of hurt whether the hurt is in the heart, mind, body, or soul.

Remember the Lord is merciful and gracious!

We have been taught **He is Jehovah-Rapha, the God Who Heals.**

Perhaps, like many of us, you have only thought of this to mean a physical healing or from a sickness. However, God desires to heal us from the heart, mind, body, or soul hurts as well.

Do you need physical healing? _____ Turn to the Lord.

Do you need soul healing? _____ Turn to the Lord.

Do you need healing in your thinking and your mind? _____ Turn to the Lord.

Do you need healing for your heart (anger, bitterness, resentment, and unforgiveness)? _____ Turn to the Lod.

Do you have a wound from a hurt that is old and deep, and the pain has never been dealt with? _____ Turn to the Lord.

Pray: *Father, thank You that You are Jehovah-Rapha, the God Who Heals. Thank You I can come to you for healing whether it is in my heart, mind, body, or soul. Today, I specifically ask You to heal my_____. Thank You for my healing and how You are merciful and gracious to us all. Father, I also ask You to heal my friend _____ for a healing in their _____. I thank You for their healing as well.*

Record in your journal how God answers your prayers.

-28-

Pleasant Words

Pleasant words are as a honeycomb, sweet to the soul, and health to the bones. (Proverbs 16:24)

Your words have power to speak life and death. Speak carefully!

Pause for a moment and read and write out Proverbs 18:21.

Pause and read James 1:19. Write this verse out as well.
It's **not pleasant** to use negative words to hurt, tear down, or to destroy people.

Ask Yourself...

Do my words hurt, tear down, and destroy people?

However, **it is pleasant** to use our words to be kind, generous, nice, gracious, polite, enjoyable, civil, delightful, and always encouraging.

Ask Yourself...

Are my words kind, generous, nice, gracious, polite, enjoyable, civil, delightful, and always encouraging?

We are to strengthen one another with kind and gentle words, to build up, encourage, and inspire others to do and be their best. This kindness offers hope to their situations by praising and complimenting progress.

Take a notebook with you today and evaluate 5 of your conversations at work and label your words as pleasant of unpleasant.

Evaluate your conversations with your family and then your friends as well.

What did you find out about yourself at the end of the day?

_____

_____

_____

_____

Using pleasant words will make your journey, more satisfying and delightful.

-29-

There Is a Process

But they that wait upon the LORD shall renew their strength; they shall mount up with wings as eagles; they shall run, and not be weary; and they shall walk, and not faint. (Isaiah 40:31)

Whatever you are undertaking at this time—your goals, dreams, plans, career, destiny, or purpose—be patient while each stage of the process is progressing.

- ✓ You have good intentions. Check.
- ✓ You have taken proper actions to bring about positive results while waiting on God's manifestations. Check.
- ✓ Now, pray and trust God in the process. Check.

Believe God will cause you to soar and be successful, in all you set your hands to do.

There is a blessing even in your waiting. Your faith is being increased and stretched to receive what is about to be released unto you.

Read Isaiah 40:31 again. Highlight each benefit of waiting upon the Lord.

But they that wait upon the LORD shall renew their strength; they shall mount up with wings as eagles; they shall run, and not be weary; and they shall walk, and not faint. (Isaiah 40:31)

While you are waiting, give the Lord thanks. Know the process is in His timing.

Pray: *Lord, thank You for this process You are taking me through. I now know You are using this process and waiting time to stretch my faith so I can receive all You are preparing to pour into my life. I want to patiently renew my strength so I can mount up with eagle's wings, run and not grow weary as I move ahead on the path and journey You have placed before me.*

Record in your journal how God's process and His timing are working in your life.

-30-

Watch What You Say

There is that speaketh like the piercings of a sword: but the tongue of the wise is health. (Proverbs 12:18)

As believers in Christ, we need to be accountable for our words and our actions. We aren't to be like the world where they say what they want even if their words are cutting, offending, and rude. They believe they have this right, under the principle of "freedom of speech" expressed in the First Amendment of the United States Constitution.

Ask Yourself...

Is this what our founding fathers really wanted our country to look and sound like?

Is this how our Heavenly Father wants us to behave toward one another?

Beware of your words and actions when you are having a moment where everything seems to be going wrong. Before you do or say something not pleasing to God, stop, take a deep breath, and pray! Others may be watching how you handle the situation. Be mindful of your attitude and mood, be careful about voicing your opinion or mindset, and watch your conduct, actions, body language, and reactions to others. Especially if it's negative.

If you were in the wrong in this situation, be quick to apologize. Demonstrate godly characteristics. Don't allow your words to be hurtful or cause pain to others. Instead, show empathy. Speak pleasant words which cause health and healing. This reflects God's goodness and His lovingkindness toward others.

Ask Yourself...

Have my words and actions been reflecting God's goodness and lovingkindness towards others?

Have I been quick to apologize when I am in the wrong?

Do I forgive quickly?

Pray: Heavenly *Father, I pray my words will continually reflect Your lovingkindness and goodness to all around me. I want to be accountable to You for my words and actions, so I please You and show the world what it means to be a believer in Jesus Christ.*

As believers in Christ, we need to be accountable, for our words and our actions.

-31-

Greater Expectations

*My soul, wait thou only upon God; for my
expectation is from Him.* (Psalm 62:5 KJV)

You can do great things when the kingdom of God is
within you.

Remember, "Greater is He that is in you, than he that
is in the world" (1John 4:4).Wake up every day expecting
something good to happen in your life.

Build your faith up to a greater dimension.

Have your attention on Christ and know He holds your
future in His hands.

Wait, expecting to receive something great.

The anointing that is upon you will usher you into your
purpose and destiny. Today is a new day. Start applying and
declaring God's principles and see His manifestations.

Start with declaring:

I am expecting something greater today!

I will wait upon You God to give me Your plan and purpose
for this day.

I can do great things because the kingdom of God is
within me.

Pray: *I am placing my attention on You, Christ. I know You
hold my future in Your hands. Please help me continually build
my faith to a greater dimension starting today. Thank You for
the anointing to usher me into my purpose and destiny.*

-32-

Established

Rooted and built up in Him, and stablished in the faith, as ye have been taught, abounding therein with thanksgiving. (Colossians 2:7 KJV)

God has ordained and established you to do great things in His kingdom. God wants to set you up permanently and forever being successful. God has equipped you with everything you need to remain in good standing with Him and your endeavors.

Keep your heart and mind fixed on the Father, Son, and Holy Spirit. If and when the winds blow, and the raging storms come, you are safe and secure. You will be able to stand.

Believe on the Lord your God, and you shall be established in Him.

Ask Yourself...

Am I being successful in my endeavors? _____

If not, ask yourself is my heart and mind truly fixed on the Father, Son, and Holy Spirit in all that I do? _____

What is the Holy Spirit showing me I need to do to achieve success God's way?

_____

_____

Pray: *Father, thank You for equipping me with everything I need to remain in good standing with You and to successfully fulfill my endeavors. I thank You that even when the winds blow, and the raging storms come, I am safe and secure. I know I will be able to stand as long as I keep my heart and mind fixed on You.*

-33-

Already in Motion

And all these blessings shall come on thee, and overtake thee, if thou shalt hearken unto the voice of the LORD thy God. (Deuteronomy 28:2 KJV)

Your blessings are already in motion. God is directing your blessings to come right to you. Our Father has already released His promises. Be ready to receive the blessings with joy and a thankful heart. Live in expectancy daily, knowing our Father knows what you need and when you need it.

If you are walking in obedience and in right alignment with His Word, your blessings are already in motion. Therefore, graciously receive everything the Father has prepared for you.

Ask Yourself...

Am I receiving His blessings? _____

Am I walking in obedience to Him and in right alignment with His Word? _____
What does this mean to me in my everyday life?

_____

_____

_____

_____

Is He asking me to make any changes?

Explain:

_____

_____

Am I receiving His blessings with joy and a thankful heart? _____

How am I expressing my joy and thankfulness to Him?

_____

_____

_____

How do I explain to others why my life is so blessed and joyful?

_____

_____

Pray: *Thank You Father, my blessings are already in motion. Thank You for directing my blessings to come right to me and already releasing Your promises. I am so thankful.*

-34-

A Different Perception

The eyes of your understanding being enlightened; that ye may know what is the hope of His calling, and what the riches of the glory of His inheritance in the saints, And what is the exceeding greatness of His power to us-ward who believe, according to the working of His mighty power. (Ephesians 1:18-19 KJV)

God has so graciously blessed you with physical sight to see. He has also blessed you with spiritual sight.

Can you see yourself through the eyes of Jesus? _____ What does that mean to you?

_____

_____

Don't look at your circumstances in the natural sense. Sometimes, in the natural things may look bleak, dark, cloudy, depressing, disappointing, uncertain, or unfavorable. As believers in Christ, you should always have a positive and optimistic attitude.

Have a different perception and see things in the realm of the spirit. See things lovely, bright, beautiful, and glowing in the light and in the sight of God.

Put a smile on your face. Now, that you have grace, mercy, wisdom, knowledge, and understanding of God's Word, your perception is clearer. Your perception is greater.

Explain what it means to have, "The eyes of your understanding being enlightened."

_____

_____

Have you discovered "what is the hope of His calling"? Explain:

_____

_____

Describe "the riches of the glory of His inheritance in the saints":

_____

_____

What does "the exceeding greatness of His power to us-ward who believe" mean in your life"?

_____

_____

It is time to let the world see you have a different perspective than the negativity of the world.

-35-

Walk Out the Scriptures

All scripture is given by inspiration of God, and is profitable for doctrine, for reproof, for correction, for instruction in righteousness. (2 Timothy 3:16 KJV)

God has already laid the foundation for those who love Him. He has given us instructions and directions to follow. The Lord will establish our thoughts as we commit our works unto Him.

Believers, we must take heed of the scriptures that constantly speak life into the hearts and minds of God's people.

How do we walk out these scriptures?

➢ We are called to continually walk by faith and not by sight.
➢ We are to walk in His righteousness to see His kingdom come on earth as it is in Heaven.

When we walk out the scriptures as ambassadors of Christ, surely others will follow.

As you spend time reading and meditating on His Word, record in your journal scriptures that help you walk as an ambassador of Christ. Memorize them and declare them as you start each day.

Also record what impact or change these scriptures bring into your life and the lives of those around you.

-36-

You Cannot Sink

SAVE me, 0 God; for the waters are come in unto my soul. I sink in deep mire, where there is no standing. I am come into deep waters, where the floods overflow me. (Psalm 69:1-2 KJV)

Life can be challenging and overwhelming at times. Cry out unto the Lord, He won't let you fall. When you go through the waters, floods, fire, storms, or your situations, circumstances, and troubles, you will not sink nor drown. Your faith will be strengthened in the Lord.

Don't get discouraged when things aren't looking right or going the way you think they should. The Lord is taking you higher. Continue to stand tall in the face of adversities. You are above the highest elevation by the Spirit of the Living God.

You will not sink when you keep your eyes stayed on Jesus.

Read Peter's story in Matthew 14:28-30.

What amazing thing did he do?

_____

_____

Why did he do it?

_____

_____

What happened when he took His eyes off Jesus?

_____

_____

What did Jesus ask him?

_____

_____

What did you learn from this story about facing the storms of life?

_____

_____

Pray: *Lord, thank You I can continue to stand tall in the face of adversities. Thank You that You have lifted me above the highest elevation by Your Spirit. Thank You I will not sink when I keep my eyes stayed on Jesus.*

-37-

Follow Me

Then said Jesus unto His disciples. If any man will come after Me, let him deny himself, and take up his cross, and follow Me. (Matthew 16:24 KJV)

We can touch more lives by being a great example of Jesus Christ. As you follow Jesus, you can love people unconditionally and lead them to Christ. Many people are hungry and thirsty for the Truth. People are tired of holding onto uncertain and temporal things. Their hearts are crying out for something sure, permanent, everlasting, lifelong, unchanging, and most of all, eternal.

God's children desire to walk in obedience to Him. They are blessed, who fear Him (Psalm 128:1).

The Lord will order our steps as we follow His ways. The Lord is saying to His people today, "Come, follow Me and live a glorious life."

What are the promises from God in Psalm 128:1-6?

_____

_____

What examples did Jesus give us that we are to follow?

_____

_____

Read these verses to describe your answer:

John 9:1-7

_____

_____

Matthew 19:13-14

_____

_____

Luke 23:34

_____

_____

Matthew 28:16-20

_____

_____

Pray: _Lord, help me to be a true follower and show me how to love Your people unconditionally, and lead them to You. Help me to set an example of Your permanent, everlasting, lifelong and unchanging love._

-38-

Life Is Priceless

For ye are bought with a price: therefore, glorify God in your body and in your spirit, which are God's. (1 Corinthians 6:20 KJV)

Jesus paid a ransom for our sins. We can never repay the Lord for His love towards us. The life we live is a "gift" from God. This is why we shouldn't take our lives for granted; but give thanks unto the Lord in and for everything.

Let's cherish this beautiful life God has given us. We can live a blessed and fulfilled life in Jesus Christ when we come to the realization, we are not our own, we belong to God. Don't allow sickness, tragedy, or calamity to get your attention before acknowledging how priceless your life is to you and to God.

Throughout each day, give God thanks. He is the Giver of life. We should live healthy, righteous, and holy lives.

The Lord has already promised His people He will satisfy them with long life and show them His salvation.

"For ye are bought with a price."
   Who paid this price? _____
   What did it cost? _____
   Does my life show Him how thankful I am? _____
   Are there changes I need to make in my attitude toward my life? _____
   Explain:

_____

_____

Ask Yourself...

Do I know what it means to "glorify God in my body and in my spirit"? _____
How would I explain this to an unbeliever?

_____

_____

Have I allowed sickness, tragedy, or calamity to get my attention instead of acknowledging how priceless my life is? _____
Explain:

_____

_____

Declare:

I was bought with a price.
I will thank Jesus daily for paying my ransom.
I will consider my life a precious gift from God.
Therefore, I will live a healthy, righteous, and holy life for Him.

Pray: *Father God, I thank You for the gift of life. Continually show me where I am not living my life the way You want me to live. Thank You for Your promise of long life. I will cherish this beautiful life until You call me home to be with You eternally.*

-39-

Unfailing Love

Know therefore that the LORD thy God, He is God, the faithful God, which keepeth covenant and mercy with them that love Him and keep His commandments to a thousand generations. (Deuteronomy 7:9 KJV)

God's love never fails. His love cannot be compared to any other gods. God's love is eternal, unfailing, and unfeigned. It will not falter nor lose its purpose. God's love is not subject to change because of any conditions or feelings.

Look up each of these beautiful scriptures describing God's unfailing love for us all. Write out and memorize the one that means the most to you today as you face life's challenges.

Say this verse out loud every day for the next week.

Then go back and choose the next verse that ministers to you and write it out, memorize it, and say it out loud for the next week.

Repeat these steps until you have completed this list. Then start your own list as you continue to read and meditate on His Word daily.

Record in your journal how this changes your life week by week.

God's Unfailing Love:

We are to love one another, as Christ has loved us. It is the Lord's commandment (see John 13:34).

Anyone who does not love, does not know God because God is love (see 1 John 4:8).

Greater love has no man than this, that a man lay down his life for his friends (see John 15:13).

God loves us and He has chosen us (see Ephesians 1:4-5).

God wants us to trust and obey Him in all things (see Psalm 33:18-22).

We can all rely on God's unfailing love (see Romans 8:38-39, John 3:16, Psalm 136:26, Romans 5:8).

Pray: *Thank You Heavenly Father for Your unfailing love for me! I love You with all my heart, my mind, and my soul.*

-40-

Cast Your Cares

Cast thy burden upon the LORD, and He shall sustain thee: He shall never suffer the righteous to be moved. (Psalm 55:22 KJV)

We cannot blame others for some of the poor choices and habits we have formed over a lifetime.

Have you fallen into this trap? _____

At times, we may not be able to stop some things from happening or have the strength at the time to cast it down ourselves. Ask the Lord for help. He can break the revolving cycle of whatever you have been dealing with in your life.

Whatever the issue may be, God is willing and able to stop what has tried to come up against you.

Take your burdens or troubles to the Lord and leave them there. He has planted your feet on solid ground, you shall not be moved.

Therefore, cast all your cares on the LORD for He cares for you (1 Peter 5:7).

How does this work?

➢ Read God's Word. It will encourage you.
➢ Rejoice in His love. It provides hope and peace.
➢ Trust in God's promises.
➢ Pray and ask Him for His help.
➢ Ask Him for the strength to overcome whatever is threatening you. Knowing He will stand with you.

Write your prayer asking the Lord for specific help you need. Thank Him for hearing your cries, and for helping. He wants to give you exactly what you need. Thank Him for your victory.

_____

_____

_____

_____

_____

_____

-41-

Are You Truly Free?

If the Son therefore shall make you free, ye shall be free indeed. (John 8:36 KJV)

Daily, confess, and declare you are free from those things holding you captive, until you are truly set free from them.

Begin by:

> ➤ Confessing out loud there are no chains or hindering spirits holding you bound.
> ➤ Confess, unto the Lord, there are no problems, situations, circumstances, or sin that has control over you, that He will not deliver you from.

Declare, unto the Lord:

> ➤ I will place every care and concern into Your hands. You are the only One who can deliver me out and set me free.
> ➤ I will abide in You, and I know, You will abide in me.

It's time for you to be free indeed! The Lord is the "Spirit" and where the "Spirit" of the Lord is, there is liberty.

Pray: *Thank You Father, as I abide in You, I am free from every bondage. I am no longer a captive. I am truly free indeed!*

-42-

Intercessors

I EXHORT therefore, that; first of all, supplications, prayers, intercessions, and giving of thanks, be made for all men. (1 Timothy 2:1 KJV)

Thank God for intercessors. They are praying and interceding for those they know and don't know. They are praying for our communities, cities, states, countries, and nations. They are praying for our spiritual leaders, as well as our government leaders.

These are prayer warriors who God has called and raised up to be intercessors. They are laying before God on our behalf, calling forth healing, restoration, deliverance, breakthroughs, blessings, and favor.

How thankful and grateful we are to have God-fearing intercessors praying for us. They pray in the spirit and are speaking directly to God. They commune with God for the needs of others to be met.

Ask Yourself...

Do I know who the intercessors are in my church family?
Do I pray for them regularly?
Do I thank God for them?
Am I called to be an intercessor?

Pray: *Thank You God, for Your faithful intercessors. Strengthen them as they intercede for Your people. Show me, Lord, if I am to join other intercessors. Please send Your Holy Spirit to guide me.*

-43-

Live There

And He said, "My Presence shall go with thee, and I will give thee rest." (Exodus 33:14 KJV)

No matter where you are, live in the sweet presence of the Lord.

Find a place in His presence, rest and linger there.

Where is this place in your life?
Go there right now.

Take rest from your labor and from your coming and going. It is time to live in the comfort of His bosom, wrapped in His loving arms. Live in the calmness and the quietness of the presence of God.

Are you willing to give God your time to receive the refreshing in your mind and soul?

If you are having problems sleeping and it seems like you are wrestling for sleep, get in the presence of the Lord, and you will find your resting place.

There is a refreshing, a peace, and a rest that comes from being in the presence of God. You don't have to walk around weary and discouraged. You can live in the rest of Almighty God.

Declare:

I will daily allow my mind, body, and soul to take up residence in the very presence of God, and rest in Him.

Pray: *Thank You Father, for Your very presence in my life. My heart, mind, and body desire to take up residence in Your presence every day of my life.*

-44-

Get Understanding

Wisdom is the principal thing; therefore, get wisdom: and with all thy getting get understanding. (Proverbs 4:7 KJV)

You may not always know or understand what God is doing in the different seasons of your life. Seek Him diligently, and He will make it plain for you.

> Trust in the LORD with all thine heart; and lean not unto thine own understanding. In all your ways acknowledge Him, and He shall direct your paths (see Proverbs 3:5-6).

Go ahead and tell the Lord you don't understand the place you are in at this moment, but you are going to trust His plan. Stay in the presence of the Lord and clarification will come. Patiently wait on God. You will be able to discern those things that are good and righteous and what is unacceptable in the sight of God.

Learn of His ways, commandments, principles, concepts, and His percepts.

Read Proverbs 9:10, 2 Timothy 2:7, and James 1:5.

How does the Bible say you get understanding?

_____

_____

Ask Yourself...

Am I truly seeking wisdom and understanding from God?

Am I trying to do things my own way and only go to God when I can't figure things out?

Pray: *Father, please forgive me for doing things my own way first, and seeking Your way only when my way fails. Please continually remind me to seek wisdom and understanding through Your Word and the guidance of the Holy Spirit.*

-45-

We Believe

But as many as received Him, to them gave He power to become the sons of God, even to them that believe on His name. (John 1:12 KJV)

We believe Jesus Christ is the Son of God, and He gave His life as a ransom for the sins of this world.

We believe the enemy has already been defeated, and God's children have the victory.

We believe the Father wants the best for His children.

Even those things we cannot see in the natural realm we believe it by faith.

We believe in healing, deliverance, breakthroughs, miracles, signs, and wonders.

We believe in the awesome power of Almighty God.

We believe all things are possible with God.

We believe in the Word of God and everything He has spoken. It is done!

We believe in the Father, Son, and the Holy Spirit.

Ask Yourself...

Do I believe the things listed above?

If so, make them your daily declarations.

Back up each of these declarations with at least one scripture and be prepared to explain to others why you believe it.

Make a copy of this page and carry it with you so you can be ready to explain your beliefs, especially to unbelievers.

Pray: *Thank You, God, for Your written Word that gives me the foundation for my beliefs and for the truths I need to share with others, especially unbelievers. Use me, Lord, to present my beliefs with boldness and confidence.*

-46-

Better Not Bitter

Because Thy lovingkindness is better than life, my lips shall praise thee. (Psalm 63:3 KJV)

Embrace life as it comes and find the good even in a bad situation. We shouldn't lean on our own understanding. We must consult the Lord.

Oftentimes, carnal thinking will keep people bitter and not better. Think about this statement for a minute.

God's Lovingkindness
Is Better Than Life

Right now, there should be praise on the inside of your heart because of His amazing lovingkindness. Our Heavenly Father wants us healthy inside and out. He wants His children living better, thinking better, eating better, doing better, resting better, seeing better, etc. Live your best life better, and do not allow bitterness to get a foothold.

Read out loud or Sing, these praise Psalms. Perhaps do one in the morning before you head out for your day and see how your days stay better and not bitter.

Psalm 145:1
Psalm 146:2
Psalm 40:3
Psalm 65:8
Psalm 150:6
Add your own favorites to this list.

Record in your journal the impact of beginning your day with giving praise to God.

Pray: *I praise You, Heavenly Father for Your lovingkindness and mercy. I am so grateful for Your forgiveness and great love. May my mouth continually praise You for Your goodness, Your grace and Your mercy.*

-47-

Wounded for Me

But He was wounded for our transgressions,
He was bruised for our iniquities:
the chastisement of our peace was upon Him;
and with His stripes we are healed.
(Isaiah 53:5 KJV)

If you have experienced any pain, suffering, mental health illness, sickness, or disease, I have some good news to share with you. Jesus bore your sins and sickness on the Cross. Therefore, you're already healed. The only action required of you is to believe and receive His Word by faith. According to your faith, you are made whole (see Matthew 9:29).

The Lord is a **Healer.** He heals any form of sickness or disease. He can and He will restore His people's health back unto them even greater than before.

He Is Jehovah-Rapha!
The God Who Heals.

Read these reports of Jesus healing.

What does each one tell you about Jesus and healing?

Matthew 8:2-3, 13 _____
Matthew 9:29-30 _____
Matthew 15:28 _____
Luke 17:12-19 _____
Mark 3:5 _____
John 5:8-9 _____

Pray: *Thank You, Lord Jesus, for willingly taking those stripes for our healing. I believe I am healed in Your name.*

Declare your healing not your sickness.

-48-

Heaven on Earth

A good man leaveth an inheritance to his children's children, and the wealth of the sinner is laid up for the just. (Proverbs 13:22 KJV)

God has called His sons and daughters to live the abundant life. God did not intend for the wicked and sinners to have His abundance. He said in Psalm 37:9, "Evildoers shall be cut off, and those who wait upon the Lord, they shall inherit the earth." God will do a miraculous transfer for those who are His.

Are you ready to live a life filled with all spiritual blessings?

Remain faithful and do the will of God. Then you will have heaven on earth, enjoying the blessings, promises, provisions, and manifestations of God.

Ask Yourself...

Am I ready to live a life filled with all God's blessings and experience heaven on earth? _____

If your answer is no, why not? _____

What does experiencing heaven on earth mean to you?

_____

_____

Read what Jesus said in Matthew 6:9-10.

What did He say it meant?

_____

_____

Pray: *Thank You Father, we can experience heaven on earth according to Your Word.*

-49-

Live in Hope

*And thou shalt be secure, because there is hope;
yea, thou shalt dig about thee, and thou shalt take
thy rest in safety.* (Job 11:18 KJV)

Even when you cannot see it in the natural; still hope for it. At least when you have hope you are saying there is a chance something good can happen. So, anticipate, be hopeful, be expecting, and be aiming for something to take place. Train your mind to live in hope and expectancy. When you live in hope, you have less room to have doubt, fear, and the feeling of giving up. Allow hope to take up residency in your heart and mind. Keep trusting in the Lord. Things will turn out for the best.

**Be optimistic, be confident, and be hopeful, in
Jesus' name!**

Read Romans 12:2.
How are you to train your mind?

_____

_____

Read Philippians 4:8.
What else are you to do to train your mind?

_____

_____

Read Psalm 1:2.
What more should you do to train your mind?

_____

_____

Why is it so important to train your mind and control your thoughts?

_____

_____

Declare:

Even when I cannot see it in the natural, I will still hope for _____.

I will anticipate, be hopeful, be expecting, and be aiming for something positive to take place today.

I will train my mind to live in hope and expectancy.

Pray: *Thank You Father, I can put my hope in You. Thank You, Lord for being my light, my strength, my song, and my hope.*

-50-

Refined

And I will bring the third part through the fire, and will refine them as silver is refined, and will try them as gold is tried: they shall call on My name, and I will hear them: I will say, It is My people: and they shall say, The LORD is my God. (Zechariah 13:9 KJV)

You may go through the fire in times of testing. Some pressure may be necessary to get God's best results in your life. Acknowledge the Lord and trust His Word.

Hold on, you are being refined, you are being freed from your impurities and unwanted elements. Impurities are being removed by the process which you are experiencing.

You are getting rid of fear, doubt, unforgiveness, depression, oppression, insecurities, and unbelief. It can be a slow process. Nevertheless, trust God to deliver you from those things hindering, delaying, or preventing your spiritual growth. God's people are refined, and they shine brightly.

You are a light, and you illuminate the light of Jesus.

Ask Yourself...

Have I been refined by God? _____

What impurities are being removed by this process?

_____

_____

What have I learned about myself that needs to be changed?

_____

_____

What is the first step I am going to take?

_____

_____

Pray: *Thank You God, for Your refining process. Please strengthen me as I submit to Your process. Show me what I need to do to become a light and illuminate the light of Jesus in my life.*

Deal With Me Lord

For all have sinned and come short of the Glory of God. (Romans 3:23 KJV)

Ask Yourself...

Can I see where I have fallen short and not given God my all?

Examine yourself carefully and determine what you can do better.

_____

_____

Am I repeating the same acts and getting the same results? _____

Stop leaning on other people's understanding and start acknowledging the Lord. He will direct your path.

Read Proverbs 3:5-6.

Declare out loud:

I will trust in the Lord with all my heart and not lean on my own understanding. In all my ways I will acknowledge Him, and He will direct my paths.

Work on improving yourself as you work on your own salvation.

Read Philippians 2:12.
Describe what this means to you:

_____

_____

Ask Yourself...

Have I done what I knew was wrong in the sight of God and failed to do what I knew to be right? _____

Read Romans 6:23.
Fill in the blanks.
"The wages of sin is _____ and the gift of God is _____ _____ life in Christ Jesus our Lord."

Pray: *Thank You Lord for being merciful and forgiving. Deal with me and guide me so I might glorify You in all I say and do.*

-52-
Stop Struggling With it

For the LORD thy God, will hold thy right hand, saying unto thee, Fear not; I will help thee. (Isaiah 41:13 KJV)

What are you struggling with today? _____

You can ask the Lord to remove everything clouding or hindering your thoughts, keeping you from walking in victory. You can turn that situation over to the Lord. You do not have to struggle with it anymore. In God's sight, that problem, situation, or circumstance is but a light affliction.

Throughout the day, confess God is in control of your life. Trust the Lord with your whole heart. You don't have to struggle anymore.

Declare:

> ➤ God, You are in control of my life.
> ➤ The struggle is over now!
> ➤ I will trust the Lord with my whole heart!

Pray: *Lord, I ask You to remove everything clouding or hindering my thoughts and anything keeping me from walking in victory. I turn this situation over to You. Thank You I do not have to struggle with this anymore!*

-53-

Pray For All

Confess your faults one to another, and pray one for another, that ye may be healed. The effectual fervent prayer of a righteous man availeth much.
(James 5:16 KJV)

In these perilous times, we all stand in need of prayer. There is much evil, hatred, jealousy, wickedness, crime, destruction, unrighteousness, and disobedience in our world. Thank God for prayer! Prayer changes the atmosphere. Those problems, troubles, situations, and circumstances will begin to shift and turn around instantaneously. That's how your Heavenly Father works. He hears your prayers, and He answers.

Pray for All humanity and for all nations.

Remember, prayer can reach people in places which seem unreachable.

The effectual fervent prayer of a righteous man availeth much.

Define "effectual fervent prayer":

_____

_____

_____

_____

Write an effectual fervent prayer for someone God is asking you to pray for.

_____

_____

_____

_____

Record this in your journal, then, if possible, follow up with this person and ask how God answered your prayer for them.

-54-

Heaviness Removed

Heaviness in the heart of man maketh it stoop: but a good word maketh it glad. (Proverbs 12:25 KJV)

If you know someone who is facing a trial or some difficulties, will you be the one who will pray and encourage them? Once they realize they do not have to face this hardship alone, their strength will be renewed.

God has sent you to strengthen those who are weighed down by life's circumstances. Some people need someone to listen to them. Give them your listening ear. When they begin to release the heaviness of their heart, it should be a ton of pressure being released off them.

God knows what His people will go through. By the grace and mercies of God, He will remove the heaviness off the hearts of His people.

There are many ways we can help others deal with heavy hearts. List the ones mentioned above:

_____

_____

_____

_____

Think of some other ways you can be God's hands, mouth, arms, and ears for those in need.

_____

_____

_____

_____

Pray: *Father God, please show me who You want me to help strengthen and encourage today. Allow me to be Your ministering friend to them today.*

What People Think of You

Be ye not deceived: evil communications corrupt good manners. (1 Corinthians 15:33 KJV)

Children of God do not get caught up on what others think of you, or what they believe you can and cannot do. Their thinking is not relevant to the plan and purpose God has in store for you.

Separate yourself from anyone who doesn't have your best interest at heart. Remove yourself from those who may have a selfish or jealous spirit.

Surround yourself with people who love God and want to genuinely see you at your best. Connect with other Believers who are living a God-fearing life. Spend time with those who are setting good examples of being Christ like and practicing what they preach.

Do not connect with anyone who will pull you down. Always connect with those who will uplift you.

Read these verses from Proverbs concerning choosing friends wisely. Record what each one advises us to do.

_____

_____

Proverbs 12:26
Proverbs 22:24-25
Proverbs 17:17
Proverbs 18:24
Proverbs 27:9

Pray: *Father God, please teach me to choose my friends wisely so they help me serve You righteously.*

-56-

Having a Difficult Day

My brethren, count it all joy when ye fall into divers temptations; Knowing this, that the trying of your faith worketh patience. (James 1: 2-3 KJV)

When you are having a challenging day and it seems like nothing is going right, find a place of strength in your heart and count it all joy. It's in those difficult times, the Lord sees what's in you. Stop in your tracks and call on Him. Your situation is just temporary.

Therefore, no matter how your day started, you can rejoice! Shake off those things trying to shift or move you off, course.

Ask Yourself...

In those difficult times of my life, what does the Lord see in me?

_____

_____

Many of the psalms speak of how David handled difficult times in his life. Read and record David's advice in each of these Psalms:

Psalm 3:1-3

Psalm 27:4

Psalm 43:5

Psalm 71:14

Sing: "This is the day the LORD has made, we will rejoice and be glad in it." (Psalm 118:24)

When I am having a challenging day, I will look in the mirror and say out loud to myself:

> ➤ I will find a place of strength in my heart and count it all joy.
> ➤ I will stop in my tracks and call on Him.
> ➤ I will confidently declare this situation is just temporary.

Pray: *Thank You, Father, no matter how my day started, I can rejoice in You! Remind me to turn quickly to You and shake off those things trying to shift or move me off the course You have for me.*

-57-

Nothing Will Keep Me Down

Wherefore seeing we also are compassed about with so great a cloud of witnesses, let us lay aside every weight, and the sin which do so easily beset us, and let us run with patience the race that is set before us, (Hebrews 12:1 KJV)

The enemy tries to place stumbling blocks in the way of God's sons and daughters. This is mainly because he knows God has great things for His children. When God's people take back their power, dominion, and authority, nothing can weigh or keep them down. Allow the Holy Spirit to strengthen you with power, then nothing can keep you down or in bondage, or hinder the work of the Lord.

The Holy Spirit has empowered you to rise with power, purpose, and provision.

Now is **not** the time for you to get discouraged, but it's time for you to be encouraged.

Ask Yourself...

What does 1 Peter 5:7 invite me to do?

_____

_____

Philippians 4:6 also says, I should

_____

_____

In Psalm 55:2,2 David writes,

_____

_____

Declare out loud:
Nothing will keep me down!

-58-

Day Dreamer

And the LORD answered me, and said,
Write the vision, and make it plain upon tables,
that he may run that readeth it.
For the vision is yet for an appointed time,
but at the end it shall speak, and not lie:
though it tarry, wait for it;
because it will surely come, it will not tarry.
(Habakkuk 2:2-3 KJV)

You are a dreamer and a visionary. You have dreamed or daydreamed about becoming successful in every area of your life. You pictured your future as God sees it.

Now it's time to write the vision down.

_____

_____

_____

_____

Are you amazed at the visions, and how brightly you see your future?

You have the unction: to do something different and amazing. It is time for you to go with the flow!

Pray: *Holy Spirit, please lead and guide me as I walk out God's plan for my life. Help me get ready to launch new creative ideas no one has thought of at this present time.*

Dream Big!

-59-

Stability

Therefore, my beloved brethren, be ye steadfast, unmovable always abounding in the work of the Lord, for as much as you know that your labour is not in vain in the Lord. (1 Corinthians 15:58 KJV)

Stability plays an important part in our lives. We can waver like the wind in our thinking and actions sometimes. Life may be overwhelming and difficult at times but keep the faith. It will get better.

Define stability:
What is the opposite of stability?
Would you say your life has stability? _____

Why or why not?
It is good to have stability to stand and endure the tests of life.

Seek God for stability, safety, and for His security to make sound decisions. Be still and wait on, the Lord. He is concerned about you and the choices you make.

**Continue to labor, be fruitful,
and stay planted in good soil.**

-60-

All Things Are Possible

And Jesus looking upon them saith, With men it is impossible, but not with God: for with God all things are possible. (Mark 10:27 KJV)

When trials come or things seem to look uncertain, believe by faith ALL things are possible with God.

Tell yourself:

➤ When God says all, He means all!
➤ By the power and Spirit of the living God whom I trust and serve, He can do the impossible.
➤ God can open doors no man can shut, and He can shut doors no man can open.
➤ I may be limited in my own strength, but when I put my faith in the hands of the Lord, I will watch the Lord do the miraculous!

Continue to obey the Word of the Lord and watch Him move mountains. In this season, keep trusting and believing God for the things your ears have heard and your eyes have seen.

What are you trusting and believing God for today?

_____

_____

Record in your journal how God does the miraculous in your life.

_____

_____

At What Cost

*"And whosoever doth **not** bear his cross, and come after Me, **cannot** be My disciple."* (Jesus in Luke 14:27 KJV emphasis added)

Ask Yourself...

What does it cost me to love and trust God? _____

Will I fully surrender unto the Lord and follow Him? _____

Do I trust the Lord enough to obey His word? _____
Will I continue to praise and honor Him when I am faced with difficult times? _____

Will I bear my own cross to be a true and faithful disciple of Jesus Christ? _____

It will cost you something to follow Christ. You may lose some friends along the way. They may not understand your God-given assignment.

Have you lost some friends because you have chosen to do what it takes to be a disciple of Jesus? _____

In your lifetime, you may go through some trials.

What kind of trials have you faced as you have lived your life as a disciple of Jesus?

Don't be alarmed, remain faithful and hopeful in the Lord. Jesus said, "If you abide in My word and follow Me you are truly My disciple" (see John 8:31).

Explain what it means to you to abide in God's Word:

_____

_____

Pray and ask the Lord to give you the strength to remain faithful and hopeful in Him.

-62-

Love Much

Beloved, let us love one another, for love is of God, and everyone that loveth is born of God and knoweth God. He that loveth not knoweth not God; for God is love. (1 John 4:7-8 KJV)

The love of Jesus is unconditional and fulfilling. His love is genuine, pure, honest, sincere, true, straightforward, and authentic. No one and nothing can be compared to His love.

His love is much needed in the world today, especially when we see so much hatred, animosity, destruction, and devastation taking place.

We are ambassadors of Christ. We must spread and disperse His love.

Describe the duties of an ambassador of Christ. (Read 2 Corinthians 5:20, John 17:16, Acts 1:8.)

_____

_____

_____

Allow the love of Jesus to shower you as you have love for one another.

In order to do this, what do you need to do?

_____

_____

Pray and ask the Lord to reveal to you how to become a true disciple and be His witness throughout your area of influence.

Record what He reveals to you.

_____

_____

_____

_____

-63-

Tired of the Cycle

We are troubled on every side, yet not distressed, we are perplexed, but not in despair. Persecuted, but not forsaken, cast down, but not destroyed. (2 Corinthians 4:8-9 KJV)

People of God, it is time to get fed up with going through the same old cycle and coming out with the same results. It is exhausting seeing others whom you love or know personally keep going through repeated cycles and not having any joy or change in their lives.

It's time to speak faith and declare 2 Corinthians 4:8-9 over those you know and love.

Decree and Declare:

- ➢ They will come out of cycles of addictions.
- ➢ They will come out of cycles of unhealthy relationships.
- ➢ They will come out of cycles of debt, lack, and living from paycheck to paycheck.
- ➢ They will come out of cycles of poor decision making.
- ➢ Those days of struggling are behind them.
- ➢ They can look forward to brighter days ahead.
- ➢ They belong to God and bondage is a thing of the past.

I speak peace, healing, deliverance, change, blessings, and favor over myself and those I know and love.

Pray: *Father, I thank You that even though I have experienced trouble, distress, been persecuted, and been cast down, I have*

Your blessings of peace and favor over my life and the lives of my loved ones. I know You are telling me it is time to get fed up with the same old destructive life cycles and seek Your way of handling anything the world sends my way. I will do things Your way!

-64-

When The Enemy Atttacks

Behold, I give unto you power to tread on serpents and scorpions, and over all the power of the enemy, and nothing shall by any means hurt you. (Luke 10:19 KJV)

The enemy is on the attack because he doesn't want God's people to reach their God-given potentials. He wants God's children to settle for less and stay in bondage to him. Put the enemy under your feet. God has empowered His people to rise above the attacks and stand firmly on His Word. Know that when the enemy comes in like a flood, the Spirit of the Lord will lift up a standard against him (see Isaiah 59:19).

Activate Your Power and Authority

1. **Trust God**, no harm can overtake you, nor will any disaster come near you.
2. **Plead the blood of Jesus** over yourself, your family, and your situation.
3. **Remind the enemy**, Jesus has already defeated him, and because of this you have the **victory**!

Read 1 John 3:8.

Pray: *Thank You Father God, for the power to tread on serpents and scorpions, and over all the power of the enemy. I know nothing shall by any means hurt me. Thank You Jesus, I can plead the blood You shed on the cross over my life. I know You have already defeated my enemy and I can stand in victory against him!*

-65-

No Longer Scarred

Who His own self bare our sins in His own body on the tree, that we, being dead to sins, should live unto righteousness: by whose stripes ye were healed. (1Peter 2:24 KJV)

Jesus suffered for our sins when He was nailed to the Cross, and because our Savior suffered in agony, we don't have to. However, out of a grateful heart unto God, we should die daily to sin. Also out of a thankful heart, we should live in hope and righteousness for Christ's sake.

Though you are probably familiar with what happened the last few days of Jesus' time here on earth, take a few minutes and review Matthew Chapters 21-27.

Record your insights from these chapters and how Jesus' sacrifice affects the healing of your scars.

_____

_____

_____

_____

_____

There are those who may have scars or marks from their past. Not to minimize anyone's pain or the tumult they had to endure, I come to encourage and tell them the scars of their past can no longer hold them bondage. Jesus paid the ultimate price for their healing of scars whether they are visible or invisible.

Declare:

> ➤ The scars of my past **can no longer hold me in bondage.**
> ➤ **I release those scars of** _____
> (hurt, physical or emotional pain, unforgiveness, physical abuse, sexual abuse, verbal abuse, adultery, divorce, or other).
> ➤ **By His Stripes I Am Healed!**

-66-

Recommit

Commit thy works unto the LORD, and thy thoughts shall be established. (Proverbs 16:3 KJV)

Sometimes we become so busy with life, we get, slack in our own commitments. It's a simple fix. Recommit and be faithful to what you need to accomplish.

Your Recommitment Check List

Check off the ones you need to work on.

☐ If you have been neglecting your family, recommit yourself.
☐ If you have fallen short in your giving, recommit.
☐ If you have been slothful on your job, recommit and become better.
☐ If you have taken a break longer than you intended from school or college, recommit to it.
☐ Most of all, recommit to spending quality time with the Lord and seeking His face.

List the ways you are going to recommit for each one you checked off.

_____

_____

_____

_____

The Lord will establish, provide, and supply you with everything you need as you recommit your life to His ways.

-67-

Train Your Mind

*For who hath known the mind of the Lord, that
he may instruct him? But, we have the mind of
Christ.* (1 Corinthians 2:16 KJV)

Desire the mind of Christ. It is very important to think like
Christ and follow His ways. We should love the way Christ
loves and treat everyone with compassion. For some, this may
not be an easy task.

Read Philippians 3:10-20.
Explain how this applies to your life's journey right now.

_____

_____

Daily work towards having the mind of Christ. Having
the mind of Christ, we will be able to understand His truths
and revelations. There is always more room for spiritual
growth and learning His teachings, thoughts, and ways.

Read what Jesus said in John 8:32.
Explain how this applies to your life's journey right now.

_____

_____

Diligently study Jesus' teachings. The Holy Spirit is a
great teacher, He dwells inside of us. He will bring things back
to our remembrance what Jesus taught and about what God

has said in His Word. The Bible instructs and teaches godly principles on how we are to be like Christ.

Read John 14:26.
Explain how this applies to your life's journey right now.

_____

_____

Also, with having the mind of Christ, we can accomplish those things, which Jesus accomplished.

Read John 14:12-14.
Explain how this applies to your life's journey right now.

_____

_____

-68-

On Your Knees

That at the name of Jesus every knee should bow, of things in heaven, and things in earth, and things under the earth. (Philippians 2:10 KJV)

When you bow down to pray and worship, you're reverencing the Lord.

Define reverencing the Lord:

_____

_____

There are times when life situations and circumstances will cause you to constantly stay on your knees and petition God for guidance and strength. Don't wait until trouble comes, pray without ceasing.

Read 1 Thesslonians 5:17.
How can you do this?

_____

_____

Read James 5:16.
What does praying fervently mean?

_____

_____

How ever you choose to pray, pray fervently to your Heavenly Father. You can pray on your knees, whisper a prayer while sitting or standing on the job, while you are driving, or cleaning your house.

What other ways and times have you found to take the time to pray, worship, and reverence the Lord even if you cannot get down on your knees?

_____

_____

You have the opportunity to give thanks and acknowledge the Lord at any time and any place.

Ask Yourself...

How often do I kneel to pray?

-69-

Don't Compare

And He said unto them, Take heed, and beware of covetousness, for a man's life consisteth not in the abundances of the things which he possesseth.
(Luke 12:15 KJV)

When you see your neighbor gaining material goods, don't despise them. You don't know their struggles or what it took for them to possess their material goods. God has already promised you, if you would delight yourself in Him, He will give you the desires of your heart.

Read Psalm 37:4.
How do you delight yourself in the Lord?

_____

_____

Rejoice when you see your neighbor or neighbors being blessed. Don't be in competition with them. Be happy for them. Remember, your purpose is not attached to what you can possess in material goods.

Purpose in your heart to do the things which please the Lord.

As you walk through your day, look for ways to please the Lord by doing things for others.

Ask God to use you to help others.

At the end of the day, record in your journal what you did and thank God you were given those opportunities.

Know if God did it for your neighbor, He will surely bless you!

As you continually seek to serve God and others, watch for the amazing ways He brings you the desires of your heart. Remember to record them in your journal. Refer to them often.

70

Listen to the Lord

My sheep hear My voice, and I know them, and they follow Me. (Jesus in John 10:27 KJV)

Don't listen to the enemy because he has nothing to say that's useful or meaningful. The enemy's job is to keep you bound and in bondage. He also wants to keep you in fear and keep you dwelling in your past. The adversary wants you to stay stuck.

Ask Yourself...

What has the enemy been whispering in my ears?

_____

_____

Have I found myself dwelling in the past? _____

What thoughts have been causing me to be distracted by fear?

_____

_____

When you listen to the Lord, you cannot be tempted to do unlawful and ungodly things.

Read Isaiah 55:2-3.
How important is it that you listen to the Lord according to these verses?

_____

_____

Read the words of Jesus in:
In Matthew 7:24, Jesus said,

_____

_____

In Mark 4:24, what did Jesus say about paying attention to what He was teaching?

In Luke 11:28, Jesus said you are blessed if you

Be thankful unto God, He has anointed the ears of His people, and they know His voice.

Listen to the Lord and be attentive to what the Spirit of the Lord is saying to you in this hour.

Find a quiet place, ask Him to give you guidance and direction each day, and then devote yourself to listening for God's voice. Record what you hear in your journal.

What do you hear Him telling you to do?

_____

_____

What is the first step you must take to obey His voice?

_____

_____

71

Excited About God

*I **was** glad when they said unto me, "Let us go into the house of the LORD."* (Psalm 122:1 KJV)

You should develop a great passion for God, to the point of being in awe of His greatness. Be excited about *who God is*.

Read Deuteronomy 5:6-10.
   Who is God?

_____

_____

   Be excited about God's lovingkindness and His compassion towards you. Get excited about your Creator, and how He spoke everything into existence. He is an amazing and awesome God.

   What excites you about God?

_____

_____

   Get excited about having a terrific place to worship and fellowship with other Christians.

Read Hebrews 10:19-25.
   Do you have a place to worship regularly?

_____

_____

Be excited that God didn't take His hand away from you when you were disobedient.

Write down a time you have been disobedient, and how God was gracious to you.

_____

_____

Get excited, it's a new day, the Lord has allowed you to see. Get excited to know God sent His only begotten Son, JESUS CHRIST, to take away your sins and the sins of the world. Get excited about God's goodness, greatness, and unconditional love.

-72-

Growing Stronger

*That Christ may dwell in your hearts by faith;
that ye, being rooted and grounded in love. May
be able to comprehend with all saints what is the
breadth, and length and depth and height: And to
know the love of Christ, which passeth knowledge,
that ye might be filled with all the fullness of God."*
(Ephesians 3:17-19 KJV)

Your faith is increasing because you are rooted and
grounded in the things of God. When you plant seeds of
love, hope, joy, peace, godliness, holiness, and righteousness,
you are growing stronger.

Read Philippians 4:8. List things that fall into these categories.

_____

_____

Grow in the Lord and be strengthened in your heart and
mind.

_____

_____

What is the best way to do this?

_____

_____

_____

Believe by faith you are growing stronger in the Lord as you turn your will over to His will. Believe you are increasing in strength and power. Be strong in the Lord, and in the power of His might.

How does one increase belief?

_____

_____

You are growing stronger, exceeding, and excelling in everything that pertains to God.

-73-

Try Again

And let us not be weary in well doing: for in due season we shall reap, if we faint not.
(Galatians 6:9 KJV)

Don't become complacent or discouraged, allowing your dreams to die. If you attempted something for the first time, and it didn't work out, try it again.

Name a time you abandoned a dream because it didn't work out. How did that make you feel?

_____

_____

_____

You may have to try repeatedly until you make progress in that area. The most elite person has attempted their goals numerous times and had failed attempts, but it didn't stop them. They continued to persevere until they saw their efforts paying off.

Read Galatians 6:9. What is our role in perseverance? How does God persevere toward us?

_____

_____

_____

Ask the Lord for His wisdom and insight. Don't procrastinate, give up, or quit. Keep moving forward. You are going in the right direction. God will give you the tools you need to reach your goals. You have the right plan and strategy. Don't lose hope. Try again. God will show you His amazing plans for your life.

Pray that God will give you the strength to persevere in whatever he has given you to do (parenting, teaching, learning, serving, etc.).

-74-

Don't Judge

"Judge not, that ye be not judged. For with what judgment ye judge, ye shall be judged, and with what measure ye mete, it shall be measured to ye again." (Jesus in Matthew 7:1 KJV)

Let's pray for one another as we walk this path with the Lord on our side.

Pray: *Lord, have mercy on [NAMES].*

God's people should not speculate, assume, or be judgmental towards one another.

Read Matthew 7:1-5.

As God's sons and daughters, we are to demonstrate God's love and His tender mercies towards one another.

Read John 13:34-35. What are some ways you can show love to others?

Do not pass judgment on someone else but consider your own ways. Be responsible for your own actions, conduct, and deeds, and see if they are in alignment with the Word of God. Let God judge the hearts of people. Let God be your JUDGE!

List things in your own life that you need to change. Commit before God not to judge others when you see them doing the same things!

Don't Stand for a Lie

A faithful witness will not lie, but a false witness will utter lies. (Proverbs 14:5 KJV)

Everything that is written in the WORD of God is truth. Anything that is contrary to the WORD or doesn't line up with the WORD is a lie.

Read 2 Timothy 3:10-17. Practice comparing things you've heard about God with what you've read in Scripture. Do they line up?

_____

_____

_____

_____

_____

Believers do not stand for lies. Don't be deceived! You know all too well God's WORD is true and He cannot lie. There are some manmade laws that are contrary to God's word. The enemy is busy trying every tactic to get people to follow him. Do not fall for his lies and deceitful ways. You know the devil is a liar and the father of lies. Stand on the WORD of God, and you will not go wrong. He is your Heavenly Father, "All Truth" and "All Righteousness."

Read John 8:42-47. Forewarned is forearmed. You know the Devil is a liar — so resist him! But never try to do so in the strength of your own power. Call on the name of Jesus, and he will depart from you.

What are some lies the Devil has told you? How do you know they're lies, and what can you do to resist them?

-76-

Be Comfortable

So God created man in His own image; in the image of God created He him; male and female He created them. (Genesis 1:27 KJV)

You are the apple of God's eye. Be comfortable in your own skin. Be the best You God has created you to be. Don't compare yourself to others. It's okay if you are different. God designed each of us uniquely.

Read Psalm 17:6-9. *What are some ways you are unique?*

_____

_____

_____

_____

God is the Potter, and you are the clay. He will continue to make, shape, and mold you. He has created you for His purpose and glory. Be who God has called you to be.

Who has God called you to be? What is your purpose in life?

_____

_____

_____

God's children will look, act, and think differently, and it's okay. Be comfortable in your own body. God loves you. Be yourself.

Read 1 Peter 2:9-10. Christians are not called to "fit in" or be just like everyone around them in the world. *How can you set yourself apart as the Apostle Peter calls us to do without attracting attention to yourself, or acting unnaturally?*

-77-

He Is God Regardless

Before the mountains were brought forth, or ever Thou hadst formed the earth and the world, even from everlasting to everlasting, Thou art God. (Psalm 90:2 KJV)

God is unchanging, He is eternal, and He is from everlasting to everlasting. Despite our situations, circumstances, problems, trials, ups and downs, disappointments, good and bad experiences, He is God.

Ask Yourself...

Do I trust God for everything? _____

Do I believe that He is in control? _____

Do I still try to keep control of things in my life? _____

If so, what are some of the things I try to control?

Nothing dictates who God is. He is God, and God alone. Our God is infinite in power, love, wisdom, goodness, peace, and truth. God is good all the time. Regardless of what people may think, how they feel, or what they may believe, God is still God, regardless.

Read Psalm 46.

Pray: *Sometimes I'm scared, Lord. I know that you are all-powerful and that you are Love itself. Please come to me and comfort my fears. Show me your love and help me to pass it on to everyone I meet.*

-78-

One Accord, One Mind

*Fulfil ye my joy, that ye be like-minded, having
the same love, being of one accord of one mind.*
(Philippians 2:2 KJV)

The church is the body of Christ, to come together
corporately and worship in unity.

*Read Hebrews 10:24-25. When was the last time you went
to church?*

_____

It's time for the people of God to work together in harmony,
seeing things as God would see them, showing the same kind
of love towards one another which the Lord has shown to us.

Read 1 John 2:9-11.

Read Philippians 4:2-3.

*Are you aware of any conflicts in your church? How might
you go about helping to resolve them in the spirit of 1
John 2:9-11?*

_____

_____

_____

_____

We are to have the mind of Christ and allow the Lord to direct our thoughts and ways as we stand together, united. Being of one mind, having compassion for one another, loving each other, being tenderhearted, being courteous, not returning evil for evil, not criticizing, but knowing that we were called so that we may inherit a blessing.

Read Philippians 2:5-8. What are the characteristics of the mind of Christ that the Apostle Paul encourages us to adopt?

_____

_____

_____

_____

-79-

Are You Connected?

And Jesus came and spake unto them, saying, "All power is given unto Me in heaven and in earth." (Matthew 28:18 KJV)

Are you connected to a power source? Do you have a relationship with the Father, through His Son, Jesus? It's time to be connected to the greatest power source, GOD. He has unlimited power available.

God is All-Powerful (Omnipotent), we can only access that power through His Son, Jesus Christ. Is it possible to disconnect yourself from that power? If so, what are some of the ways you have done this, and how can you reconnect?

Are you connected to God's power source to receive a surge of His power, anointing, and strength? Surround yourself with godly people of great influence, those who are empowered from on high. Get connected with people who can push you into your destiny. There are people of influence who can see the greatest in you that needs to be birthed out of you. There is a greater power dwelling on the inside of you. Stay connected to JESUS!

Read Mark 16:15-18.

What is the authority that Christ gives in these verses?

_____

To whom is he giving this authority?

_____

Can we obtain this authority as well, and if so, how?

_____

-80-

Live Purposefully

See then that you walk circumspectly, not as fools but as wise. Redeeming the time, because the days are evil. (Ephesians 5:15-16 KJV)

Time is valuable. Therefore, let's not waste it doing nothing.

Checklist: How have you wasted valuable time?

- ☐ Spending too much time online.
- ☐ Gossiping about others.
- ☐ Avoiding church.
- ☐ Not helping someone clearly in need.
- ☐ Sinful activity.

Don't live foolishly, unwisely, and carelessly, but be wise, mature Christians. Let's live on purpose! Be determined and maximize your time reaching those goals and achieving them.

What are some ways you can put the time you have to good use?

_____

_____

_____

_____

If you don't know what your purpose is at this present moment, seek the Lord for His purpose, plan, and will for your life to be revealed. Jesus has given His children gifts, talents, abilities, and opportunities to do great things. Have a personal relationship with God for your spiritual, financial, mental, and physical growth. Allow your life to be meaningful. LIVE ON PURPOSE!

Read Proverbs 20:13. Apply this to a variety of contexts in your life and discover how you can stop "loving sleep."

-81-

The Solution

Looking unto Jesus the Author and Finisher of our faith; who for the joy that was set before Him endured the cross, despising the shame, and is set down at the right hand of the throne of God. (Hebrews 12:2 KJV)

The answer to any problem is Jesus. When you have Jesus on the inside of you, He goes before you. He is making those crooked places straight and those rough places smooth. There are no problems, obstacles, mistakes, disappointments, difficulties, circumstances, situations, or troubles that the Lord cannot fix.

What problems are you facing right now? List them below, and for each one answer whether you've given it over to God yet.

_____

_____

_____

_____

The Lord knows your end from your beginning. He is on the throne of God working things out in your favor.

Read Hebrews 4:16. What does it mean for Jesus to be on the throne of God? Is there any problem he isn't able to resolve?

Put your trust in the Lord and He will see you through any trial. Try Jesus—He is your solution.

Read John 14:13-14. Do you truly believe this? What difference would it make in your life believed these words of Jesus when you make your requests known to him through prayer? What sorts of things should you ask Him for?

_____

_____

_____

-82-

A Quality Decision

I will bless the LORD, who hath given me counsel: my reins also instruct me in the night seasons. I have set the LORD always before me: because He is at my right hand I shall not be moved. (Psalm 16:7-8 KJV)

It is necessary for Christians to lean, depend, and rely on God. Making a quality decision is going before the Lord and seeking Him diligently for His answer to your needs. Seek Him first, not as a last resort.

Jesus instructed us to "seek first the kingdom of God and his righteousness, and all these things will be added to you" (Matt. 6:33). What are "all these things"?

_____

_____

_____

You shouldn't wonder or guess if you have made the right decision or not. Spend time in prayer and wait for your answer. The Lord will speak to your heart. He will speak to you audibly.

What does the voice of God sound like when he speaks to you? How do you know it is really Him, and not someone or something else?

_____

_____

_____

He will also give you confirmation through His word, or through one of His delegated authorities.

Read Romans 15:8-9. *What is the purpose of God confirming His Word?*

_____

_____

Remember, before making any decision, first go to the Lord in prayer.

What are some situations in your life that you have not yet brought to the Lord in prayer?

We Are The Church

Now ye are the body of Christ, and members in particular. (1 Corinthians 12:27 KJV)

On this journey, we may have encounters with strangers and unbelievers. This is our opportunity to act as Christ's representative in the earth.

Read Hebrews 13:2. Have you ever had an encounter like this? How did you respond?

_____

_____

_____

Believers, we carry the anointing and power to speak life into the hearts of those who are hurting and lost. We are the righteousness of God. We are the body of Christ.

The body has many parts. Which part of Christ's body are you?

_____

_____

Be aware. There are many people waiting on us to hear what God has to say through His sons and daughters.

Do. Witness and minister to that hurt, pain, disappointment, bondage, struggle, and grief.

Remind. *Let* the hurting person know that Jesus loves them, that He has not forgotten about them. All of us are important to God. We all have a part in the body of Christ. We have a great responsibility to win souls to Christ.

Whom are the people in your life that you have not yet shared Christ with? How might you go about doing so?

_____

_____

_____

- 84-

Every Day Is A Day Of Thanksgiving

Giving thanks always for all things unto God and the Father in the name of our Lord Jesus Christ. (Ephesians 5:20 KJV)

You have so much to be thankful for.

Make a list of all the things you have to be thankful for. **Pray** *and thank God for them!*

_____

_____

_____

_____

God has given you, life, and life more abundantly. He has given you strength, and the mobility of your limbs. You are in your right mind to comprehend and discern what is good and evil. He has given you His grace and mercy. He has blessed you in so many ways.

Read Deuteronomy 2:7. What wilderness have you passed through? How did God bless you in the midst of it?

_____

_____

_____

You're thankful and grateful for God's unmerited favor.

Show God how grateful you are by blessing someone else!

Reverence God every day with thanksgiving.

What does it mean to reverence God? Make a practice of thanking Him for something every day.

Pray: *Lord, you have given me all things. I do not deserve any of them, but you look after my every need. Thank you with my whole heart, and do not take your Holy Spirit from me.*

-85-

Kindness

In a little wrath I hid My face from thee for a moment; but with everlasting kindness will I have mercy on thee, saith the LORD, thy Redeemer. (Isaiah 54:8 KJV)

Kindness is a very good quality to have. To act with kindness means you are friendly, generous, and concerned for others and their well-being.

Showing kindness doesn't have to be elaborate. What is one simple way you can show kindness to someone today? (Hold the door open for someone, make breakfast for your spouse, etc.)

_____

_____

Some characteristics of kindness are generosity, affection, charity, courtesy, gentleness, goodwill, goodness, grace, hospitality, patience, thoughtfulness, and understanding.

Can you name a Bible character who exhibited one of each of these characteristics?

_____

_____

Kindness has many benefits: it increases happiness, improves health, improves relationships and connections, and reduces stress.

Read Matthew 25:31-46. Think about the consequences of not showing kindness!
Demonstrate love and kindness to all of mankind. Kindness is a fruit of the Spirit.

What are the other Fruits of the Spirit? (Galatians 5:22-23)

-86-

A Vow

Better is it that thou shouldest not vow, than that thou shouldest vow and not pay. (Ecclesiastes 5:5 KJV)

Have you ever made a vow to the Lord that you didn't keep? Many have said, "Lord, if you get me out of this, I promise not to do such-and-such again."

Read Matthew 5:33-37.
Have you ever promised God something that you didn't follow through on? What was it, and why didn't you follow through?

_____

_____

When the Lord gets them out of the very thing. They asked Him to rescue them from, they sometimes go right back and do the same thing again. Therefore, they didn't keep their promise, nor their word. They were desperate for some relief, and they may have meant it, but oh, how quickly they forget.

Read Jeremiah 18:15.
What can you do to keep the memory of God strong in your heart?

_____

_____

When the Lord rescues His people from their troubles or despairs, they should keep their word. God's people shouldn't make vows or promises they don't intend to keep.

God is the great keeper of promises. What promises does He keep?
(Read Isaiah 41:10.)

_____

_____

_____

_____

Reach Out

But whoso hath this world's goods, and seeth his brother have need, and shutteth up his bowels of compassion from him, how dwelleth the love of God in him? (1 John 3:17 KJV)

Christians, we should have a heart of compassion, able to reach out to help someone in need. The Lord has blessed us with the means and resources to reach out to those who are struggling, hurting, lacking, broken, and misused. All of us can do something!

Read Hebrews 13:16.
Who do you know in need of help?

_____

_____

We can reach out and help those in need of our assistance. It may be our money, our time, our wisdom, or our knowledge. It may be our advice or counsel, our resources, or something as small as a ride to the grocery store or the bank. Think about what you have, and what you are not using.

Giving Checklist
Check off the things you give:

- ☐ Time
- ☐ Money
- ☐ Food

- ☐ Clothing
- ☐ Hospitality
- ☐ Friendship
- ☐ Other _____

It could be a blessing to someone else. Christians, we are not selfish people. We are cheerful givers! Take the time to see who you can help today. It will bless your soul!

-88-

Fasting

And it came to pass, when I heard these words, that I sat down and wept, and mourned certain days, and fasted, and prayed before God of heaven. (Nehemiah 1:4 KJV)

If you have been diligently seeking God's face and have not heard from Him, try fasting. What are you willing to do or give up, in order to hear the instructions and revelations of God?

What are things other than food that you can give up to God in order to hear from Him?

_____

_____

_____

Fast and **pray**, and abstain from food, drinks, and other things which often take your attention.

Set aside time for prayer and fasting. Fasting is a great way to humble yourself in the sight of God.

Read Matthew 6:16-18.
Think of ways you can fast without attracting attention to yourself.

_____

_____

_____

Fast and pray, focus on reaching the heart of God. Seek the Lord through fasting and praying to know His will for your life.

Jesus fasted for forty days in the wilderness, but we need to be careful not to attempt more than we can actually accomplish without harming ourselves. Try fasting for just a few hours at first, or maybe for one meal. Or, try going without certain types of foods: dairy, meat, or sweets. Work up to more. Always accompany your fasting with prayer, and God will sustain you!

-89-

Whatever The Dilemma Is

And call upon Me in the day of trouble; I will deliver thee, and thou shalt glorify Me. (Psalm 50:15 KJV)

Whatever your dilemma is, God can fix it. Place that situation or circumstance, which seems so difficult for you, into the Master's hands.

What situations are you facing that seem insurmountable?

_____

_____

Know there is nothing too hard for God. Don't let this thing move you away from God, but let it move you closer to Him. Believe and trust God for His end results.

Read Luke 1:37.
What is the context of this verse? If God can do that, what can He not do for you?

_____

_____

God can handle anything which puts pressure on you or causes you to be distraught. Whatever your dilemma is, release it to the Lord and begin to praise Him! He has already worked it out for you.

Read 1 Thessalonians 5:16-18.

Think of times God has delivered you from difficult circumstances that seemed impossible to you. Then, think of situations you're currently facing, and instead of worrying, thank God for them and give Him praise. See what He will do for you, and then praise Him some more!

_____

_____

_____

-90-

Bless Someone

Every man according as he purposeth in his heart, so let him give; not grudging, or of necessity: for God loveth a cheerful giver. (2 Corinthians 9:7 KJV)

Who has God laid on your heart to bless? Will you be obedient and bless that person or institution?

Take a moment to write at least five people or institutions (churches, charitable organizations, etc.) that you can bless in some way.

_____

_____

In what ways can you bless them? (Financial support, prayer, volunteer work, taking food to a family in need, etc.)

_____

_____

Ask the Holy Spirit to lead you and show you who to bless. It is such a tremendous blessing when you can bless someone. God sees your heart.

Read Acts 20:35.

I challenge you to bless someone, and see the joy overtake them, and yourself as well. It is a blessing when you consider others above yourself. This act of kindness and gratitude is important to God. He can trust you to love and look out for someone else's needs. Give with a joyful spirit!

Read 2 Corinthians 9:7.
What keeps you from giving cheerfully? What can you do to make it easier to do so?

_____

_____

Bless someone, because your heart knows it's the right thing to do.

Don't Make Hasty Decisions

Trust in the LORD with all thine heart; and lean not unto thine own understanding. In all thy ways acknowledge Him, and He shall direct thy paths. (Proverbs 3:5-6 KJV)

Sometimes we make hasty decisions based on our emotions and operate out of the flesh. However, we should take a minute to consult God. He will give instructions and sound doctrine.

Read John 16:12-15. **Pray** to Holy Spirit to help you understand God's Word, and to guide your life in a way that will be pleasing to God and good for your health: mentally, physically, and spiritually.

The Holy Spirit will steer us in the right direction, to make good and timely decisions. Mistakes are made when we make hasty decisions. Go to the Lord in prayer and wait patiently for Him.

Read Philippians 4:6. *Make a list of things you would like to talk to God about or ask Him for and commit to praying for each of them every day.*

The Lord will allow His people to make good and timely decisions.

Commit to God not to do anything without consulting Him first. He may answer you right away, or He may not; He may answer in a way you're expecting, or He may answer you in a way that is totally unexpected. Prepare yourself for whatever may come by drawing closer to Him in prayer and Bible reading.

Read 1 Kings 19:9-18. *What does this mean for how God communicates with us? How are you going to make yourself ready to hear whatever word He has for you?*

-92-

Higher In The Lord

The righteous shall flourish like the palm tree: he shall grow like a cedar in Lebanon. Those that be planted in the house of the LORD shall flourish in the courts of our God. They shall still bring forth fruit in old age; they shall be/at and flourishing. (Psalm 92:12-14 KJV)

You have been dedicated and faithful. Now God is calling you higher. You have increased in your faith, wisdom, knowledge and understanding. God is elevating you higher because there are souls to be won. He is also calling you higher, to speak life to a hurting, lost, and dying world.

Read John 4:27-38.
The fields are ripe for harvest! Who can you share the wonderful news of the Gospel of Jesus Christ with? Make a list:

_____

_____

_____

The Lord is taking you higher in the Spirit realm. He will show you great and mighty things which are to come. He is calling you higher because He wants to fulfil His purpose, plan, and will through you. The Lord has planted you to flourish and to prosper in all levels of ministry.

Read Jeremiah 29:10-14.

Do you find this encouraging? What Babylon has God rescued you from, and what have you done to thank Him?

_____

_____

God is elevating you higher to advance the kingdom. The Lord is taking you higher because He is calling GREATER for your life. Greater connections, influences, love, peace, favor, visions, power, anointing, wealth, health, walk, talk, and **prosperity**.

Holy Grounds

And He said, "Draw not nigh hither: put off thy shoes from off thy feet, for the place whereon thou standest is holy ground." (Exodus 3:5 KJV)

Where are you standing? Are you standing on holy ground?

Read Exodus 3:5.
Have you done anything to make yourself and your surroundings holy?

_____

_____

Is your home on holy ground? Does the presence of the Lord reside there?

Read 2 Samuel 7:27-29.
Have you asked God to bless your house, and everyone in it?

Is the foundation where you worship holy? Do you know the ground where you worship is sacred? Are you loved and connected to God there? Hopefully, your church and home are where the presence of God is heavy, and His presence saturates the place.

Read Acts 2:42-47.

How does God reward the Church in Acts for their faithfulness?

_____

_____

Hopefully, you are standing on holy ground. The foundation is solid, and the presence of the Lord abides there always. You can encounter His Glory there.

-94-

No Matter What

I will praise Thee, O Lord my God, with all my heart: and I will glorify Thy name for evermore.
(Psalm 86:12 KJV)

Sometimes life's issues can press you down, and it feels like all your energy is drained. But open your mouth and say, "No matter what, Lord, I am going to give you praise, and I'm going to honor you with the fruit of my lips."

Ask Yourself...

Are you in the habit of praising God for <u>everything</u>?

_____

_____

Where do you get your strength?

_____

_____

Praise God all the time. No matter what it looks like, no matter how hard it may seem. No matter how long your dry spell has lasted. No matter what has come, and now is gone. No matter what you have done or didn't do. The Lord is saying to you today, "Don't worry yourself."

Read Matthew 6:25-34.

How has God met your needs throughout your life? How can you make a habit of trusting Him for everything?

_____

_____

_____

Trust Him, and He will see you through it all. God is a loving, caring, and forgiving God.

-95-

No Shortage

For the LORD thy God hath blessed thee in all the works of thy hand: He knoweth thy walking through this great wilderness: these forty years the LORD thy God hath been with thee; thou hast lacked nothing. (Deuteronomy 2:7 KJV)

The Lord has made this precious promise: He will supply all your needs, according to His riches in glory through Christ Jesus. There is no shortage in the kingdom of God. GOD IS INCREDIBLE!

His supply will never run out. Those who seek the Lord will lack no good thing. You will not go without. Your provision is already prepared. God has so much stored up for you. You will not be able to contain it all. There is no shortage, only unlimited resources made available for the people of God.

Read Luke 6:37-38.
What role do you have to play in receiving from God?

_____

Lack Forgiveness Checklist
Who do you need to forgive? Check all that apply.

☐ Parents
☐ Siblings
☐ Children
☐ Spouse
☐ Coworkers
☐ Neighbors

☐ Friends

There is no lack for His wisdom, knowledge, understanding, favor, provisions, promises, love, peace, joy, righteousness, blessings, manifestations, and revelations.

-96-

Grateful For Friends

Iron sharpeneth iron; so a man sharpeneth the countenance of his friend. (Proverbs 27.17 KJV)

To have friends in your life, you must show yourself friendly. It is good to have Christian friends to enjoy, share your thoughts with, confide in, pray with, travel with, and for support during difficult times.

> **Read** Proverbs 17:17 and 18:1.
> What are the characteristics of a good friend? Do you demonstrate those to others in your life? Do you make room in your life for others?

_____

_____

_____

It is also a blessing to have friends who have lived a long life, who can impart wisdom and knowledge to you.

Read Proverbs 13:20.

Have you made a conscious decision to foster good friendships? Are there any negative relationships in your life right now that you need to break free from?

_____

_____

_____

Know, a true friend will love you at all times, through the good and the bad. They will be by your side when you need them the most. Those are the friendships you can treasure. If you do what He has commanded you, you are a friend of God. He knows your faith, and your righteous living. He calls you, "FRIEND."

Read Proverbs 18: 24. Who is the author of this verse talking about? Do you have that Friend in your life?

-97-

Don't Complain

Let no corrupt communication proceed out of your mouth, but that which is good to the use of edifying, that it may minister grace unto the hearers. (Ephesians 4:29 KJV)

If you realize you are complaining, stop, and redirect your thoughts.

Ask Yourself...

What have I complained about today? _____

In the last week, have I gone a whole day without complaining? ____

Where do complaints come from? _____

Why is complaining dangerous? What can it lead to? _____

Count your blessings. Do they outweigh the negatives? _____

When facing each day, be mindful of your conduct, of how you engage in communication with others. Encourage and build each other up in the faith and grace of Jesus Christ. There is no need to complain, but there **is** a need to be grateful and thankful daily.

Why is it important to be grateful? Does it really make a difference in our day-to-day lives?

_____

_____

_____

Don't complain about your problems. Give them to the Lord. Don't complain about others. Pray for them. Show more gratitude and mercy. Don't complain, God has been so good to you.

Read James 5:13-20.
What would the world be like if everyone did this? Use your imagination!

_____

_____

_____

-98-

Pure Prayer

And this is the confidence that we have in Him, that, if we ask anything according to His will, He heareth us: And if we know that, He hears us, whatsoever we ask, we know that we have the petitions that we desired of Him. (1 John 5:14-15 KJV)

We must go to the throne of grace with a sincere heart without trying to impress God with eloquent words. We shouldn't bribe or beg God for anything we need. Our Heavenly Father knows how to take good care of His children. He wants His sons and daughters to have clean hands and a pure heart before Him. Seek the Lord in prayer with a sincere heart. He is listening, and He will answer your requests.

Read Matthew 6:5-7 and Daniel 6:10-11.
What do these passages indicate is one of the most important aspects of prayer that is pleasing to God? Where can you pray?

_____

_____

Spend more time in prayer, thanking God for His goodness and His lovingkindness.
How much time can you set aside each day, morning, and evening?

_____

_____

Acknowledge and reverence the Lord in prayer.
Make a list of God's attributes; thank and praise Him for each one.

_____

_____

Go to God with a thankful and grateful heart.
Each day, find at least one thing to thank Him for.

Let your heart first be pure, so that your prayers can pierce the heart of God.

-99-

The Only Way

Jesus saith unto him, "I am the way, the truth, and the life: no man cometh unto the Father, but by Me." (John 14:6 KJV)

Disobedience has led people to some dark and cold places, to which they had no intention of traveling. Many have heard and rebelled against God's Word.

What are some dark, cold places you've ended up by straying from the Lord and His desire for your life?

_____

_____

_____

They have heard His Word repeatedly, but decided to disregard His word and His ways, only to find out that their own ways were temporal. However, if they had chosen God's way, things would have turned out better. His ways are righteous and fruitful.

Can you think of some Bible stories about people who chose their own way and ended up in misery? Look them up and list the passages here.

_____

_____

_____

Jesus Christ is the only Way. He is The Way, the Truth, and the Life. Jesus Christ is the mediator between God and mankind.

Read John 14:6-7.

Ask Yourself...

Do I really trust Jesus completely?
Do I really believe there is no way to God but through Jesus?
What does it mean that Jesus is the Way, the Truth, and the Life?

-100-

Your Testimony

And they overcame him by the blood of the Lamb, and by the word of their testimony. And they loved not their lives unto the death. (Revelation 12:11 KJV)

Sharing your testimony could impact the lives of so many people.

Write your life story, focusing on how you came to Jesus. Use it to help you talk to others about your faith. Think about sending it to a magazine or online blog so more people can see it and benefit from it!

Because you went through much turmoil, you can offer others hope. The good news about this is that you went through it, and God delivered you out of it. With your testimony, others can be exempted from making some of the same mistakes you made.

Read Proverbs 21:11.

What are some mistakes you've made? Think about the ways you made them right and write them down. Do you know anyone currently making the same mistakes? How can you offer them guidance in a loving way?

_____

_____

_____

_____

It is only by the grace of God and His lovingkindness that those life experiences did not kill or destroy you. Keep blessing mankind by telling your testimony. Someone is listening!

Have you ever been helped by hearing another person's testimony? What were some particular points that you found especially helpful?

-101-

Know Your Rights

And He said unto him, "Thou hast answered right:
this do, and thou shalt live." (Luke 10:28 KJV)

You are the righteousness of God.

Read 2 Corinthians 5:21.
You have the right to love God with all your heart, soul, strength, and mind. Sons and daughters of God, know that you have the right to praise and worship the Lord in the beauty of His holiness.

Read Mark 12:29-31.
What does it look like to love God in this way? How close to/far away from this are you?

_____

_____

_____

The Holy Spirit dwells in you, you have the right to encourage and build others up in the faith. Because you are converted, you have the right and the privilege to strengthen your brothers and sisters in Christ.

Read 1 Thessalonians 5:11.
Who do you know that you can build up in Christ? In what ways do they need to be encouraged?

_____

_____

Continue to share and spread the Gospel of Jesus Christ. Live a blessed and meaningful life.

Declare:

- I will live in the blessings the Lord has given me.
- I will live every day, every minute, every hour with meaning.
- I will live and speak the Gospel to everyone I meet.

-102-
Charge Your Angels

For He shall give His angels charge over thee, to keep thee in all thy ways. (Psalm 91:11 KJV)

The Lord has given His angels charge over you.

Read Matthew 18:10.
Reflect on what it means, God loves you so much that He has given you a guardian angel, and that angel is always in His presence in Heaven.

_____

_____

_____

_____

Charge your angels to work for you because you walk in authority and power. Therefore, put your angels on assignments. They are here to keep you safe and protected. The angels of the Lord encamp around those who fear Him, and He commands His angels concerning you, to guard and protect you.

Read Psalm 34:7.
Using an online concordance or Bible site (like www. BibleGateway.com), find other references to the Angel of the Lord. Who is this angel?

_____

_____

Meanwhile, let's be loving and kind when we encounter strangers, because we could be entertaining angels unaware.

Read Hebrews 13:2.

It is so important that we treat everyone with kindness and love. Be on the lookout today for one person you can show some form of hospitality to (giving them food, helping them with a task, saying a kind word). Try to find someone you normally wouldn't have any interaction with, or someone you don't know at all.

-103-

Don't Blame God

They kept not the covenant of God and refused to walk in His law; And forgot His works, and His wonders that He shewed them. (Psalm 78:10-11 KJV)

If you choose not to do things God's way, don't blame Him when troubles come. Swallow your pride and take ownership of your bad judgment.

Pray: *Forgive me, Lord, for doing things my way, and not Yours. If I have caused harm to anyone, show me so I can ask their forgiveness and set right what I have done wrong. Help me to remember You and Your commandments at all times, so that I never fall into the snare of the evil one, or cause harm to anyone. Amen.*

When things are not going your way, or unexpected things begin to happen, do not blame God. When situations take longer than you had hoped, stop to consider whether you may be the hold-up, because of your disobedience.

Ask Yourself...

Have I willfully or knowingly broken any of God's commands? _____

Have I formed habits that lead to destruction?

_____

Do I blame God for difficult situations? _____

Am I blind to my own faults and shortcomings?

_____

If you answered yes to any of these questions, think of ways you can begin to overcome these habits.

Take responsibility for your actions. Look to the Lord whenever you need help. Heed His Word.

Read Hebrews 4:11-13.

Commit to reading the Word of God every day. Keep a journal to note the changes it makes in your life.

-104-

Vengeance Is the Lord's

*Dearly beloved, avenge not yourselves, but rather give place unto wrath: for it is written, **vengeance is mine; I will repay**, saith the Lord.* (Romans 12:19 KJV, emphasis added)

When someone does you wrong, don't lie or spread rumors. Don't interfere or try to get revenge, allow God to fix it. Allow the Lord to fight your battles.

Read Romans 12:14-21.
Has someone treated you badly or unfairly? What good can you do for that person?

_____

_____

_____

Whatever thoughts you were having about getting back at the person who hurt you, pray and let it go. It's not godly to pursue payback.

Sometimes it can be helpful to imagine what may have happened in someone's past, or even earlier that day, that led them to hurt you. Did their car break down? Did they have to take their child to the emergency room? Maybe they didn't even realize what they did or said hurt someone else. Try writing some possible scenarios.

_____

_____

_____

_____

_____

This is not your character, and it does not represent who you are in Christ. Leave it alone, allow God to handle it His way. No real peace can come from taking challenging matters into your own hands. But place your cares and concerns in the Lord's hand. "VENGEANCE IS MINE, I WILL REPAY, SAYS THE LORD."

-105-

Give Them To The Lord

For this child I prayed; and the LORD hath given me my petition which I asked of Him. Therefore, also I have lent him to the LORD; as long as he liveth, he shall be lent to the LORD. And he worshipped the LORD there. (1 Samuel 1:27-28 KJV)

Do not tolerate the enemy messing with your children, niece, nephew, godchild, or grandchildren.

Read Mark 10:13-16.
What can you do to guide the children in your life to Christ?

To-Do Checklist:

☐ Read Scripture to them
☐ Help them learn to pray
☐ Take them to church
☐ Teach them a hymn or praise song
☐ Enroll them in Vacation Bible School

Stand on the covenant you made with God when you gave your child back to the Lord. The enemy must take his hands off of God's children. The responsibility of parents is to love their children and care for them and share the love of Jesus Christ with them. We must also correct and redirect them when we see them headed in the wrong direction.

Read Proverbs 13:24 and 29:17.

We show our children love by reprimanding them when they do the wrong thing. What happens when children are never disciplined? Whose fault is that?

_____

_____

_____

Let's place our children in the hands of God; He will build a hedge of protection around them.

Everything By Faith

That your faith should not stand in the wisdom of men, but in the power of God. (1 Corinthians 2:5 KJV)

Everything in this season of your life will come by faith. Believe and trust God for it. Be diligent, and do not give up during the waiting process.

Decree and Declare:

> ➤ I will put my faith in God entirely.
> ➤ My strength comes only from the Lord.
> ➤ There is nothing God cannot help me overcome.
> ➤ God cares about me more than anyone else does, including myself!
> ➤ When I am waiting in God, it is not a burden.
> ➤ God will come to my aid when I ask Him.
> ➤ I will overcome through Christ who gives me strength.

Seek God's face in fasting, prayer, and study of His Word. Understand that God is faithful and just. He hears the heartfelt cries of His children. By faith, believe and receive everything the Lord has spoken to you in His Word. Everything you have believed God for shall come to pass and remain. Stand faithfully, firmly, and confidently.

Pray: *Dear God, You, know how hard it is to wait. Sometimes it seems like nothing will ever change: Please help me, and if I have to wait longer, please give me the strength to do so without* *complaining or growing bitter. Send Your grace upon me and grant me your peace.*

Try thanking God for what you *do* have, instead of thinking about what you don't have. Sometimes simply thinking about something else has more effect than we could ever imagine!

-107-

Creativity

For we are His workmanship, created in Christ Jesus unto good works, which God hath before ordained that we should walk in them. (Ephesians 2:10 KJV)

What are your creative abilities? The Lord has blessed His people to be creative, talented, and gifted.

God Himself is so creative He made an entire universe for His children to live in and enjoy.

What are some creative pursuits you've always wanted to get better at? Check all that apply.

☐ Painting
☐ Drawing
☐ Writing poetry
☐ Storytelling
☐ Singing
☐ Playing an instrument
☐ Acting
☐ Gardening
☐ Cooking
☐ Other _____

Look at it this way: the Creator has given His children creativity to demonstrate their God-given abilities at home, in the workplace, at school, in their communities, and in their churches. Discover what your creative abilities are and begin operating in them, because you have received salvation and been made one with Christ. Discover what your creative abilities are. You were created to do great and mighty things.

Creativity Challenge: Pick one thing that you checked off on the list above and commit to practice it at least three times a week. Really try to master it; read instructional books, watch tutorial videos, and get the right equipment. Make something beautiful for God!

-108-

It's Your Time

Delight yourself also in the LORD; and He shall give thee the desires of thine heart. Commit thy way unto the LORD; trust also in Him; and He shall bring it to pass. (Psalm 37:4-5 KJV)

It's your time to walk in the blessings and favor of God. Everything the Lord has promised you. He will make good. He will manifest His Word.

What does it mean for God to manifest His Word? (Read Titus 1:1-4.)

_____

_____

You have been believing, trusting, and waiting patiently for God to give you your heart's desire. The wait is finally over—He wants to bless you immeasurably! He knows your heart, and He sees your faithfulness. Receive and embrace everything the Lord wants to do in your life.

Pray and ask God to reveal what He wants to do in your life and commit to following up on what He shows you. Write down what you learned and consult it regularly so that it stays fresh.

What is some things God has done in your life already? Write at least three here:

Believe and trust God for a continual flow of His blessings, promises, and favor. Delight yourself in the Lord, and He will give you the desires of your heart.

Reflect on Matthew 6:33. What strikes you most about this verse, and how does it reflect your own experience?

-109-

Release It

And this is the manner of the release: Every creditor that lendeth ought unto his neighbor shall release it; he shall not exact it of his neighbour, or of his brother; because it is called the LORD'S release. (Deuteronomy 15:2 KJV)

Whatever you are holding onto in this season, release it and let it go. If it's causing you to lose hope or has you under stress, release it and let it go.

What are you holding on to?
- ✧ Worry
- ✧ Fear
- ✧ Resentment
- ✧ Possessiveness
- ✧ Jealousy
- ✧ Anger
- ✧ Addiction

God knows and understands everything you're going through.

Release that problem,
Release that child,
Release that spouse,
Release that debt,
Release that business,
Release the drugs,
Release the alcohol,
Release the anger,
Release the bitterness,

Release the unforgiveness,
Release the hurt and pain,
and let it go.

Release it today and receive healing, in Jesus' name!

-110-

I Dare You

I will praise Thee, 0 Lord my God, with all my heart, and I will glorify Thy name for evermore. (Psalm 86:12 KJV)

I challenge you to put God first in everything you do. I dare you to be the first to break the generational curse from your family lineage. I dare you to break any bad habits.

What bad habits do you need to break?
(Read Colossians 3:5-7, Ephesians 4:20-24.)

_____

_____

_____

I dare you to live in daily expectancy. I challenge you to obey the Lord's instructions, and to follow His directions.

Are you attuned to God's direction? Why, or why not?
(Read Proverbs 16:9; 3:5-6.)

_____

_____

_____

I dare you to bless a stranger.
What happened when you blessed a stranger? Write the story here:

_____

I dare you to start reading and studying your Bible daily. *Make time to do this, and do it faithfully for one whole week. How much of the Bible did you get through?*

I dare you to tell your children, spouse, family members, or friends that you love them. I dare you to exalt, honor, glorify, magnify, and praise the Lord.

-111-

Place of Unity

Behold, how good and how pleasant it is for brethren to dwell together in unity! (Psalm 133:1 KJV)

Unity should characterize our homes and our churches. Sadly, in some instances, this is not the case. There is chaos, confusion, turmoil, or dysfunction, and no love or peace abiding there. Each church and its members should come together in unity.

The Apostle Paul describes the Church as a body with many members (or parts). What part are you in the Body of Christ, both in the broader church and in your particular church?

(Read 1 Corinthians 12:12-31.)

_____

_____

Show others how to love and be at peace with one another. Church may be the only time when those gathered there may feel they are loved, or belong to a family. There should be a spirit of love and liberty as we come together in a corporate setting.

Read John 13:34-35.

Ask Yourself...

Would others know I am a Christian just by looking at me?

_____

_____

Is my church body loving and kind, or strict and judgmental?

_____

_____

Does my church body affect my ability to love others?

_____

_____

What can I do, given my part in the body of Christ, to encourage my brothers and sisters in the Lord to love others as Christ loves us?

_____

_____

-112-

You Changed My Life

And I will give them an heart to know Me, that I am the LORD; and they shall be My people, and I will be their God, for they shall return unto Me with their whole heart. (Jeremiah 24:7 KJV)

Know Jesus for yourself. Be the one who says, "Since Jesus came into my life, I have never been the same." Desire that intimate relationship with Him that is like no other relationship you have known.

What does an intimate relationship with God look like? (Read Psalm 73:28, James 4:8, Psalm 19:1-14.)

_____

_____

You will see your life changing for the better, as you spend quality time in the presence of the Lord. The closer you get to the Lord your heart and mind will line up with His Word.

What are some ways you can draw closer to God? Write down as many as you can think of.

_____

_____

Cry out to the Lord in prayer. You can experience a complete turnaround in your life as you put your trust in the Lord. God has all the answers you need.

Set aside some time to **Read Psalm 119** (it's long!). Write down at least five ways the author describes his life of prayer, and what his relationship with God is like as a result.

_____

_____

_____

_____

_____

-113-

Still Learning

To whom God would make known, what is the riches of the glory of this, mystery among the Gentiles. which is Christ in you, the hope of glory: Whom we preach, warning every man, and teaching every man in all wisdom; that we may present every man perfect in Christ Jesus.
(Colossians 1:27-28 KJV)

Whether you are young or old, you can always learn more about God's Word. You can learn more from studying and meditating on Scripture, which you have read repeatedly. When you study His Word, your eyes are enlightened. Your ears are inclined to hear the Lord speaking to your heart.

Read 2 Timothy 2:15 (KJV).
What can you do to go beyond just reading the Bible to actually studying it and getting the most out of it that you can?

_____

_____

God is still revealing Himself through His Word and the Holy Spirit. The Word of God is so rich and profound.

Read Hebrews 4:12.
Spend some time in God's Word. Pick a passage at random and ask God to show you what He wants you to gain from it. Write down what comes to you.

_____

_____

The Word of God will always speak life to those who are born again, and to those who desire and seek to know Him in the depths of their souls.

Read John 6:63.
In what way is the entire Bible the words of Christ?

_____

_____

-114-

Image on the Inside

I the LORD search the heart, I try the reins, even to give every man according to his ways, and according to the fruit of his doing. (Jeremiah 17:10 KJV)

When people look at you, do they see the heart and mind of Christ in you? It's pleasant when others can recognize the heart of God through the lives of His sons and daughters.

What *do* people see when they look at you?
(Read 1 Timothy 4:12-16.)

_____

_____

Allow your heart and mind to become stronger, wiser, and better in His ways and understanding. The image on the inside of you should reflect the image of Almighty God.

We know from Scripture that man is made in the image of God. What does that mean, and how can we reflect it to others?

_____

_____

Know that man looks at the outward appearance, but God looks at the heart.

Read 1 Samuel 16:7, Jeremiah 17:9-10, and Ezekiel 36:26. What is in your heart? Have you been given a heart of flesh? How can you know?

_____

_____

_____

The Father's ways are gracious, merciful, faithful, holy, righteous, godly, full of lovingkindness, gentle, meek, humble, thankful, and grateful.

-115-

Rejoice Today

Rejoice in the Lord always: and again, I say, Rejoice. (Philippians 4:4 KJV)

Whatever comes your way today, please do not dread or regret the day.

As soon as you encounter difficulties today, turn them over to God. Write down each one and actually thank God for it, as an opportunity for growth.

_____

_____

_____

You have everything to be thankful and grateful for. Do not give the enemy any satisfaction. Rejoice, for you have the peace of God surrounding you and your family. Rejoice, for you are covered by the blood of Jesus.

No matter what we encounter, God is in control of all things, and means them for our benefit. Write down one "bad" situation you've encountered that turned out for good and give thanks!

(Read 1 Thessalonians 5:16-18.)

_____

_____

Rejoice, for God has given you the strength and abilities to carry out His plan. Rejoice, for you have more working in your favor than what is trying to work against you. Your God is BIGGER than anything you could face today.

The secret to making it through the hard times is to give thanks to God, and not to blame Him for what you encounter, or give yourself credit for making it through. Write down the hardships you're currently facing and end each sentence with "<the love of God."

(Read Philippians 4:10-13.)

_____

_____

Now, start rejoicing!

Be Stimulated

And let us consider one another to provoke unto love and to good works. (Hebrews 10:24 KJV)

Be on a mission to lead and offer guidance to others who may need a little push.

Let your love for Christ encourage and energize someone else to live for and to please God.

Be stimulated, be motivated, and move in the ways and things of God.

Declare:

- ☐ I will not be stingy with what God has given me but will share it with others as I have opportunity.
- ☐ I will share the Gospel with others, and if necessary, I will use words to do so.
- ☐ I will find all my comfort in God and will fill myself to the brim with His love, pouring the overflow on others.
- ☐ All people are my brothers and sisters, and I will treat them as such.

Allow your love for God to spark or ignite that fire in others. Love on people, don't show favoritism or be judgmental. God will use you to change the hearts of others.

Pray: *Lord God, I know that you love me. Help me to let that love out, not keeping it inside, but sharing it with everyone around me. Give me the ears to hear and the eyes to see the* *needs and suffering of others and grant me the strength to meet those needs with your love. Make me a conduit for the good things You have in store for everyone!*

-117-

Take God Seriously

God is not a man, that He should lie, neither the son of man that He should repent. Hath He said, and shall He not do it? Or hath He spoken, and shall He not make it good? (Numbers 23:19 KJV)

You can take God at His Word. Because He has spoken it, He will make it good. His word will not return to Him void.

Read Isaiah 55:10-13.
In the context of this verse, what is it that God's Word will accomplish? Do we have anything to fear?

_____

_____

It must accomplish what He sent it to do. Whatever God has promised you, know that all of His promises are "Yes," and "Amen."

Read 2 Corinthians 1:18-22.
Explain what the Apostle Paul means by this.

_____

_____

_____

Stand on, His Word. Trust what God has already spoken and see Him bring it to pass. This is a guarantee—you can count on God; He is not like man.

In what other ways is God not like man? Write at least three things.

It is impossible for God to lie! When God promises His people something, He is going to do it! Trust Him!

_____

_____

_____

Read 1 Corinthians 1:9.

Memorize this verse and say it aloud whenever you're in doubt!

-118-

Stretched

For we stretch not ourselves beyond our measure, as though we reached not unto you: for we are come as far as to you also in preaching the gospel of Christ. (2 Corinthians 10:14 KJV)

Believe. You are believing God will do greater things in you, and in the body of Christ.

Acknowledge. In your spiritual walk, you are acknowledging the Lord.

Stretch and grow. You are stretching your faith as you see yourself growing spiritually and walking out the will of God.

You are speaking to those things that are not as though they were. Your faith is being stretched as you patiently wait on God.

What are you waiting for? How is God stretching you while you wait?

_____

_____

_____

_____

_____

You are stretching your faith while working diligently and faithfully on God's assignment. You are being stretched beyond your normal level of doing things.

What are you actively doing to exercise your faith?

_____

_____

Can you see any improvement in your life?

_____

_____

How would things be different if you were relying only on your own strength and wisdom?

_____

_____

-119-

A Quiet Place

And in the morning, rising up a great while before day, He went out and departed into a solitary place and there prayed. (Mark 35 KJV)

When you are trying to find a quiet place to pray, all kinds of distractions come that were not there previously. You need this quiet time and place to hear directly from God.

Read 1 Kings 19:12-13.
What has God spoken to you in the quiet?

_____

_____

Keep searching for a quiet place to pray and worship. It is okay if your quiet place must change occasionally. Some people may use their office or study. Some people may find quietness in the bathroom or a spare room in the home. For some, it may be inside their car or in their flower garden.

Write down some places you could pray in silence and try them out.
Read Matthew 6:6.

_____

_____

Do what works for you. Find your quiet place and develop an intimate relationship with God.

Read Luke 18:9-14.

What does this passage tell us about the attitude we should have in prayer?

_____

_____

Pray: *Lord, I want to know You. Help me to be consistent in prayer, and free me from the distractions that keep me from meeting You in the stillness. Let nothing in the world stand between me and You.*

-120-

A Greater Passion

And they said one to another. Did not our heart burn within us, while He talked with us by the way, and while He opened to us the scriptures? (Luke 24:32 KJV)

Have such a passion for the Word that it brings you joy as you ponder on His goodness and love for all of mankind. Allow your love for the Word of God to saturate your heart and mind.

What are things you love about God's Word? Write down as many as you can think of.

_____

_____

_____

_____

Share this passion with others. His Word is spirit, and it is life.

Consider joining or starting a Bible study. God will visit those who seek Him. What book of the Bible would you most like to study?

_____

Develop a personal relationship with the Father through His Son, Jesus Christ. Jesus is the greatest Teacher, Friend, Lord, Savior, Deliverer, Peacemaker, and Redeemer there is.

Read Isaiah 9:6-7.
Are there any other words or names you can think of to describe Jesus?

_____

_____

Read and study God's Word. Feel His love and compassion in your heart. It's a burning desire; you must tell someone about this man named JESUS!

Tell one person about Jesus today. Write about it in your journal.

-121-

No Other Name (Jesus)

Neither is there salvation in any other: for there is none other name under heaven given among men, whereby we must be saved. (Acts 4:12 KJV)

Jesus Christ is our Lord and Savior. He was crucified, and God raised Him from the dead. He is now seated at the right hand of the Father making intercessions for us.

What does it mean that Jesus is interceding for us? (Read Romans 8:31-39.)

_____

_____

There is no other name like that of Jesus. Everyone who calls on the Lord Jesus Christ will be saved.

This is a powerful promise. What does it mean to call on the name of Jesus Christ? (Read Romans 10:5-21.)

_____

_____

It's by His power that we have forgiveness of sin, that miracles are performed, and that healing and deliverance is manifested. There is no other name whereby we can have access to the Father, except through His son Jesus.

Why is the name of Jesus so powerful? Who is Jesus? (Read John 1:1-18.)

_____

_____

_____

_____

Pray: *Lord Jesus, I know You are the Son of God and God Himself. By your power, intercede on our behalf to the Father and do not let me fall into unbelief. I have faith in your Name, and I call on You to save me from my sins. Have mercy on me, Lord!*

-122-

Compel Mankind

And the lord said unto the servant, Go out into the highways and hedges, and compel them to come in, that my house may be filled. (Luke 14:23 KJV)

God has commanded His servants to go out into the hedges, highways, communities, and neighborhoods for those who are lost and do not have a relationship with Him, and to invite them into the household of faith.

Read Luke 14:12-24.
Who is the people Jesus instructs us to invite to "the great feast"?

_____

_____

If you know someone who has backslidden, continue to encourage them as God works on their heart.

Read James 5:19-20.
Who do you know that has fallen away and is in need of encouragement?

_____

_____

If you know someone in need of a good church home, where the 'Word of God' is being reverenced, acknowledged, and taught, invite them to worship with you. Someone is waiting on the invitation.

Read Proverbs 14:14.
What does it mean to be filled with your own ways?

_____

_____

_____

Read Hosea 14:1-4 and Romans 6:1-5.

_____

_____

If God loves us freely despite our backsliding, does that mean we should not worry about backsliding?

-123-

Go After It

Be ye strong, therefore and let not your hands be weak: for your work shall be rewarded. (2 Chronicles 15:7 KJV)

Go after the vision with all your, might. Be determined to go after your dreams and goals. To achieve anything in life, you must take charge and go after it.

Make a list of your dreams and goals and write a plan for each one in your journal that you can follow through on.

Being lazy, stagnant, slothful, and inactive gets people nowhere in life. Make it your priority to go after those dreams, career, promotion, or degrees with all your strength.

Decree and Declare:

➢ In Christ, I have the strength to achieve my goals.

➢ The enemy will not tempt me to abandon my dreams.

➢ As long as I trust God, He will clear every obstacle out of my way.

➢ I will not let fear of failure keep me from making progress in my life.

➢ My days of laziness and inactivity are behind me, my days of striving are ahead of me.

With God on your side, all things are possible. You will accomplish much. Take advantage of the open opportunities waiting for you. The Lord will bless the work of your hands. You shall see a great reward.

-124-

It Is Well

Run now, I pray thee, to meet her, and say unto her, Is it well with thee? Is it well with thy husband? Is it well with the child? And she answered, It is well. (2 Kings 4:26 KJV)

God is a very present help in time of trouble. Put your trust in the Lord. He won't let you down, nor will He let you fall. God is faithful, and always honors His word. Do not be troubled or discouraged by what you do or don't see happening in your life.

Ask Yourself...

What is the source of my discouragement?

_____

_____

What have I done to "turn the tables" on difficult situations?

_____

_____

Do I really believe that God is on my side? Why or why not?

_____

_____

Turn those situations over to God. The Lord has come to deliver and set the captured free. God knows all about your cares and concerns. Even before you open your mouth or go to Him in prayer, He knows. Be still and know that He is God.

Read Psalm 23.
Record all the promises God makes in this chapter. If you can, commit them to memory.

_____

_____

_____

Rest assured that your Heavenly Father will come to your rescue. Believe and announce with confidence: IT IS WELL! IT IS WELL! IT IS WELL! in my soul.

-125-

Speak Wisdom

But the wisdom that is from above is first pure, then peaceable, gentle, and easy to be intreated, full of mercy and good fruits, without partiality, and without hypocrisy. (James 3:17 KJV)

Over time, we should increase in wisdom. If you lack wisdom, ask the Lord to give you His wisdom. He has all the wisdom we would ever need.

Read Proverbs 8.
What are the characteristics of Wisdom?

_____

_____

_____

_____

When we obtain wisdom, we also obtain knowledge and understanding of the truth. Wisdom speaks loudly! Receive godly wisdom as it is poured out. Wisdom is priceless to those who take heed to instructions and counsel.

Who are some people in your life that you can gain wisdom from?

_____

_____

It's good to sit in the presence of older and wiser people, who are seasoned in the Word of God. The wisdom of their soul is heartfelt, insightful, and knowledgeable.

Why do you think older people are often wiser? (Read Proverbs 20:29 and Job 12:12-13).

_____

_____

Wisdom speaks when it is deeply rooted in others to share their faith encounters and life experiences.

-126-

Just Turn

Repent therefore of this thy wickedness, and pray God, if perhaps the thought of thine heart may be forgiven thee. For I perceive that thou art in the gall of bitterness, and in the bond of iniquity. (Acts 8:22-23 KJV)

Christians, we know that the enemy may try to plant all kinds of thoughts in our mind. If we are not careful, we will sometimes entertain those thoughts. The enemy can take his trickery, bribery, and wicked devices back to his godforsaken place: HELL.

Read John's account of the Last Supper in John 13:1-30. Note how the Devil plays on Judas' shortcomings. What are the things in your own life the Devil can use to manipulate your own thoughts, and what can you do to defend yourself?

_____

_____

_____

_____

No matter what we have done, God is a forgiving God. Repent, turn, and change direction.

Read 1 John 1:8-9.
Do you make a habit of confessing your sins to God? What will happen if we do not acknowledge our sins before Him?

_____

_____

_____

Let us walk in wisdom, knowledge, and understanding, knowing that our sins have been forgiven. We will give up sin for the sake of righteousness and for Christ's sake. We are no longer lacking in knowledge, nor will we find ourselves trapped in the enemy's snare.

Pray: _Dear God, I have sinned before You. Please forgive my sins and help me to walk according to your ways. Amen._

-127-

Praise Going Up

PRAISE ye the LORD. Praise the LORD, 0 my soul. (Psalm 146:1 KJV)

It really doesn't take much to praise the Lord, especially when you think of His goodness. He is worthy of all praise. Give the LORD your best praise! Praise Him with a song or with a dance.

Try writing a song or poem for God. Tell Him how much you love Him and think of His particular attributes that you adore!

Praise and acknowledge Him by telling Him how much you love and adore Him. Let the Lord know that He has been better to you than you have been to yourself. Just begin to Praise Him!

We should not hold back from praising God. He is the Lord and Creator of all, and the Savior of our souls! The Psalms are like the original praise songs to God. Read Psalm 150 and try to think of more ways you can praise Him than those listed there.

_____

_____

_____

Praise Him! Praise Him! Hallelujah, Lord! Glory to God! You are Worthy, Lord! Bless Your Holy and Righteous Name! Thank You, Jesus! Lord, You're Mighty! Hallelujah, Jesus!

Lord, I Magnify Your Name! There is no one greater than You, Lord! Lord, I honor You!

What can you do to praise God? Write down as many things as you can think of, and then think up some more!

_____

_____

_____

_____

_____

-128-

Seek Him

One thing have I desired of the LORD, that will I seek after; that I may dwell in the house of the LORD all the days of my life, to behold the beauty of the LORD, and to enquire in His temple. (Psalm 27:4 KJV)

Make a declaration to seek the Lord daily. You can seek Him early in the morning, at midday, in the evening, and at night. He is waiting on you.

Read Psalm 63:1.
Think of how much the Psalmist loved God! Do you love Him that much? What have you done to show Him?

_____

_____

_____

God loves when His sons and daughters spend intimate time with Him. Seek the Lord to be empowered by the Holy Spirit. Seek the Lord for clarity and instructions for your purpose and destiny. Seek Him during fasting, praying, and worshipping.

Read 1 Thessalonians 5:17.
How often should you pray? How can you do that?

_____

_____

Let nothing stand in your way, or keep you preoccupied or distracted from diligently seeking the Lord.

Ask Yourself...

Do I pray at every opportunity, or would I prefer to do other things?

Are my prayers mostly about me, or do I give thanks to God?

What do I do to encourage those around me to praise God?

-129-

Don't Be Opened to Wickedness

For the grace of God that bringeth salvation hath appeared to all men. Teaching us that, denying ungodliness and worldly lusts, we should live soberly, righteously, and godly, in this present world. Looking for that blessed hope, and the glorious appearing of the great God and our Saviour Jesus Christ. (Titus 2:11-13 KJV)

Don't accept wickedness. Carefully choose your friends. If you know your friends are doing wrong, kindly remove yourself from them. Don't agree with them to commit a crime or any ungodly act.

Is it possible to spend time with people who regularly choose to do the wrong thing and remain unaffected? (Read 1 Corinthians 15:33-34.)

_____

_____

You are the righteousness of God. Don't entertain foolishness, wickedness, deceitfulness, trickery, bribery, lying, robbery, confusion, manipulation, killing, or any other of the countless ungodly acts.

Where does sin start, and how can you defend against it? (Read Mark 7:20-23.)

_____

_____

Have the heart and mind to only do the things which will glorify God. Be open to love, peace, kindness, respect, clean hands, a pure heart, doing good, holiness, and righteousness.

Declare:

> ➤ *I will dedicate my heart and hands to God.*
> ➤ *I will be a good example to those around me, rather than being persuaded to follow them into evil.*
> ➤ *I am set apart for the Most High, and I will honor Him in all my ways.*

-130-
Your Labor Is Not In Vain

*For God is not unrighteous to forget your work
and labor of love, which ye have shewed toward
His name, in that ye have ministered to the saints,
and do minister.* (Hebrews 6:10 KJV)

People of God, know your labor has not been in vain.

What have you done for the Lord?
(Read 1 Corinthians 15:58 and Ephesians 2:10.)

_____

_____

Whatever works or deeds you have committed yourself to,
continue to give God your very best. Your deeds in the home,
job, church, and community have not been in vain. You have
diligently labored in love. The Lord will not forget your works.

What should our attitude be when we do good works?
(Read Matthew 6:1-4.)

_____

_____

Even though you had to toil through some difficulties, your
labor was not in vain. Your hard work didn't go unnoticed.
God sees your heart. God knows how faithful, willing,
dedicated, and patient you have been.

What does God promise regarding those who are faithful to the end?
(Read Revelation 3:12.)

_____

_____

The Lord will reward you greatly, and you will enjoy the fruits of your labor.

What is the characteristic of those the Lord rewards?
(Read Psalm 128.)

_____

_____

-131-

Sit At Jesus Feet

And Jesus answered and said unto her, Martha, Martha, thou art careful and troubled about many things: But one thing is needful; and Mary hath chosen that good part, which shall not be taken away from her. (Luke 10:41-42 KJV)

Sometimes we become too busy and distracted by the affairs of life and cheat ourselves out of spending intimate time with the Lord.

Your Distraction Checklist:

What distracts you from getting to know Jesus? Check all that apply.

- ☐ Friends
- ☐ Family duties
- ☐ Work or career
- ☐ Entertainment
- ☐ Hobbies
- ☐ Television
- ☐ Surfing the Internet

What can you do to minimize these distractions without, neglecting the responsibilities, you must fulfill?

_____

_____

_____

Don't miss out on the precious time to sit at the feet of Jesus. We must listen to His teachings and instructions. There are times when we serve and times when we need to sit. We should sit quietly at our Savior's feet and inquire of Him. There is so much we can learn and discover just by sitting and listening. The Lord delights in having His sons' and daughters' undivided attention.

-132-
Look Past The Natural

For we walk by faith, not by sight. (2 Corinthians 5:7 KJV)

Believers, look past what you see, in the natural. The Holy Spirit has caused you to see in the spirit realm by faith. God is revealing Himself to you and showing you in the Spirit what He has in store for your future.

What is the key to seeing with spiritual eyes? (Read Hebrews 11:8-10.)

_____

_____

Focus on things, above and not on the things on this earth. God wants to manifest His goodness and greatness, more than what we can even imagine in the natural. You cannot allow your sight to be limited to what you see in the natural but allow your eyes to adapt to what you can see by the Spirit.

Ask Yourself...

What am I currently focusing on?

What does God want me to focus on?

How do I balance the goodness of creation with the importance of devoting myself to the spiritual life?

What most often causes me to lose my focus?

What steps do/can I take to regain the proper focus?

-133-

What Are You Okay With?

For I know the thoughts that I think toward you, saith the LORD, thoughts of peace and not of evil, to give you an expected end. (Jeremiah 29:11 KJV)

Do not be okay with living a mediocre life. Demand more from yourself, and do not settle for less than God's best.

We all have many tasks in this life. How should we do them? (Read Ecclesiastes 9:10.)

_____

_____

You are not average. You are extraordinary! You are the Lord's workmanship, His handiwork, created in Christ Jesus to do good works.

Who are we serving by our good works to others? What happens if we do good for others?
(Read Matthew 25:31-46.)

_____

_____

God has given you the capabilities to access more as you increase in power and authority. He has given you power to do the impossible. Only be okay with walking out God's purpose, plan, and will for your life.

If we're honest, we all have weakness, and often feel as though continuing to do good is just too hard. What does the Bible teach us about who God strengthens? (Read Isaiah 40:28-31.)

_____

_____

_____

Pray: *Lord, I often feel as though I can't go on, that doing things Your way is just too hard. Please remind me that I am Your special creation, and that You love me and will give me the strength to do what You want me to!*

Do Your Best

I can do all things through Christ which strengtheneth me. (Philippians 4:13 KJV)

Choose to do your best. The Lord knows and sees your heart. God will not ask you to do anything too hard which He has not already prepared you for.

Sometimes we feel as though we just can't go on. Without God's help, that's probably true much of the time. Fortunately, we *do* have God's help. What does the Apostle Paul say about bearing up when the pressure is just too much?

(Read 2 Corinthians 1:8-11.)

_____

_____

_____

_____

God wants His children to be their best, do their best, and have His best for their lives. When God sees your efforts and determination, He will allow you to succeed. God will give His people the grace to do His will.

What is the source of the strength God gives to His people? (Read Ephesians 3:14-19.)

_____

_____

God's grace empowers His people to do great and mighty things for the kingdom. You must be confident in knowing you can do all things through Christ who strengthens you.

The Bible is full of stories and encounters of who did great things for the Kingdom of God. Many of those encounters are reviewed in Hebrews 11, the "Hall of Faith." You've probably read this chapter many times. Read it again, looking for the one thing that all of these "overcomers" had in common and write it here.

_____

_____

-135-

A Different Walk

Therefore, thou shalt keep the commandments of the LORD thy God, to walk in His ways and to fear Him. (Deuteronomy 8:6 KJV)

Keep the Lord's commandments and His principles. Walk in peace and confidence. Trust the Lord to order your steps and to give you a different walk.

According to Jesus, what are the commandments that God wants us to obey?
(Read Matthew 22:34-40.)

_____

_____

Acknowledge the Lord and His ways. He will make your path smoother.

Specifically, what do we need to do in order for God to make our paths straight?
(Read Proverbs 3:5-6.)

_____

_____

Walk with the Lord and hear His voice.

What does it mean to walk with the Lord?

_____

_____

He will put a spring in your step. Keep marching, keep walking by faith, and keep walking in love.

Love is the "oil" that keeps the "motor" of faith running. How important is it to walk in love?
(Read 1 Corinthians 13.)

_____

_____

_____

Start Rejoicing

Be glad in the LORD, and rejoice, ye righteous: and shout for joy, all ye that are upright in heart.
(Psalm 32:11 KJV)

Start rejoicing in the goodness of Jesus Christ because He saved your soul from Hell.

Start rejoicing, the doctor gave you a good report!

Start rejoicing that you have children, young or old, who are faithful and serving the Lord.

Start rejoicing, someone you know has been delivered from drugs.

Start rejoicing over that one soul you have brought into the Kingdom of God.

Start rejoicing over the pay increase and job promotion.

Start rejoicing, the Lord has shown you, His favor.

Start rejoicing, this is the day that the Lord has made, you will rejoice, and be glad in it!

Start rejoicing, God has provided for you, food, clothing, and shelter.

Start rejoicing, you have transportation, or you have the funds for transportation.

Start rejoicing, the LORD woke you up this morning in your right mind.

REJOICE IN THE LORD!

-137-

Vision His Word

Where there is no vision, the people perish, but he that keepeth the law, happy is he. (Proverbs 29:18 KJV)

The Word of God will bring change to any situation. God's Word gives insight into everything pertaining to His will and His kingdom. You are truly blessed if you obey His word.

To obey God's Word, you must know His Word. How well do you know God's Word? How much time do you spend in it every day?

God's Word gives fresh revelation. His Word allows you to walk in purpose, power, and promises. The Word empowers, equips, establishes, and settles you.

Because it is so central to our lives as Christians, what should our constant attitude toward the Word of God be? (Read Romans 1:16.)

_____

_____

You are truly blessed when you honor and keep God's Word alive in your hearts. Allow the Word of God to dwell deep inside of you.

When the Word of God goes in, what comes out? (Read Colossians 3:16, Luke 6:45.)

_____

God's Word is powerful, it is your lifeline. Envision God's Word as a burning torch within you. The fire in you will never go out because of His Word.

Memorize Psalm 119:105 and repeat it to yourself every morning and every evening!

-138-

He Is King

Which in His times He shall shew, who is the blessed and only Potentate, the King of kings and Lord of lords. (1 Timothy 6:15 KJV)

Jesus Christ is King. He rules and reigns over Heaven and Earth. Jesus is seated at the right hand of His Father. Jesus is supreme, glorious, and of great splendor. He is King over His Kingdom, and His Kingdom is not of this world. Jesus Christ is the Eternal King! Jesus is Lord of all.

Read John 8.
Reflect on Christ's statement, "before Abraham was, I AM."
What does this say about who Christ really is?

_____

_____

_____

Allow the Lord to rule and reign in your life, as you continue to take steps of faith in your Christian walk. Allow the Lord to rule and reign over your finances, relationships, family, your household, and your place of worship.

Christ the King Checklist:

What areas of your life do you still need to give over to Christ's control?

☐ Family

- ☐ Work
- ☐ Relationships
- ☐ Finances
- ☐ Church
- ☐ Thoughts
- ☐ Possessions
- ☐ Dreams and aspirations
- ☐ Free time
- ☐ Personal wellbeing

-139-

Spirit of Truth

This is He, that came by water and blood, even Jesus Christ; not by water only, but by water and blood. And it is the Spirit that beareth witness, because the Spirit is truth. (1 John 5:6 KJV)

Jesus, Son of the True and Living God. He gave His life so that we may live. He shed His blood at Calvary. Christ died for the sins of the whole world. He is the Savior of the world.

How can we be sure that Jesus is the Savior? (Read 1 John 4:14 and 1 Corinthians 15:1-9.)

_____

_____

_____

Witness and tell someone about Jesus, the One who saves and forgives.

Share the good news of the Gospel with someone. What did you say to them? What was their response?

_____

_____

_____

_____

Through the blood of Jesus, we now have eternal life in Christ. There is no one like Him. We also have three witnesses, the Spirit, the water, and the blood, and all three agree.

Read 1 John 5:6-8.
What does this passage mean?

_____

_____

_____

All who believe in the Son of God know in their hearts that this testimony is true.

Read John 21:24, and think about how this verse can be used as evidence to the truth of the Gospel.

You Are Not In This Alone

There shall not any man be able to stand before thee all the days of thy life; as I was with Moses, so I will be with thee. I will not fail thee, nor forsake thee. (Joshua 1:5 KJV)

The good news is that you are not in this alone. God is with you, He is Immanuel, "God with us."

Who is this verse talking about specifically?
(Read Matthew 1:23.)

_____

Even when it seems like you are going through situations alone, you're not alone! God will never leave you nor forsake you. There are people all over the world experiencing similar situations, or worse ones. God is with them, and He is with you.

Will God ever leave us to our own devices?
(Read Deuteronomy 31:6.)

_____

_____

God is OMNIPRESENT, He is everywhere, all at the same time. Be blessed, be encouraged, and know GOD LOVES YOU. You are NEVER alone.

Ask Yourself...

Do I truly believe God is with me all the time?

Do I truly believe God loves me, no matter what?

What are some other attributes of God (omniscience, omnipotence, etc.)?

-141-
Sit Under The Word

Thy word is a lamp unto my feet, and a light unto my path. (Psalm 119:105 KJV)

Make sure you are planted and established in a God-fearing church, where the Word of God is being taught.

What is your responsibility as one being taught? (Read Acts 17:10-11.)

_____

_____

God is faithful. You and your family are covered and protected by hearing and applying the truth to your lives. You and your family will reap the benefits of sitting under the Word. Dedicate yourselves, be faithful to the household of God.

Renew your commitment to God as a family. Write down what you will say as you promise God that you will follow Him together.
(Read Joshua 24:14-15.)

_____

_____

The Word will guide and show you the path you should follow. The Word is a burning light which keeps God's children safe and protected. Sit faithfully in the household of God and be spiritually fed.

It's important that the teaching we receive is faithful to the whole Word of God, and that it is sufficient to help us grow in faith and love. What are some characteristics of good teaching?

(Read 2 Timothy 2:15, Titus 2:1-15, and Jude 1-25.)

_____

_____

_____

_____

-142-
Truth Will

Be sober, be vigilant, because your adversary the devil, as a roaring lion, walketh about, seeking whom he may devour. (1 Peter 5:8 KJV)

Understand that God's Word is true, He cannot lie. Don't listen to or entertain the lies, manipulation, and bribes the enemy offers you.

What lies did the Devil use to try to convince Jesus to abandon His ministry and saving work in the world? Has he used some of the same lies on you?
(Read Luke 4:1-14.)

_____

_____

_____

Stand on the truth, live by the truth, and do not bow to the enemy's lies. Don't compromise the Truth for lies. Be watchful and prayerful, so you can discern good and evil.

We cannot be stagnant in our growth in God's Word. What does the author of Hebrews identify as the thing that will enable us to discern good from evil?
(Read Hebrews 5:12-14.)

_____

_____

Trust in the Lord and stand on His Word. The truth will allow you to be free and live a fulfilled life.

Truth vs. Lies Checklist:

What are the sources of lies in your life?

☐ *False teaching*
☐ *Media*
☐ *Unbelieving friends and family*
☐ *Unwanted thoughts*
☐ *Worldly attitudes*

-143-

Move Self Out Of The Way

Let nothing be done through strife or vainglory; but in lowliness of mind let each esteem others better than themselves. Look not every man on his own things, but every man also on the things of others. (Philippians 2:3-4 KJV)

Take some time to move self out of the way to see the needs of others. God wants to use you, and He will, as soon as you stop doing things your way and obey His command.

Ask Yourself...

Who are the people in my life with needs I can meet?

_____

_____

Do I blame them for their needs, or do I view them with love and compassion, seeking ways to help them rise above their situations?

_____

_____

How am I getting in the way of God's ability to use me?

_____

_____

Do I practice putting myself in other peoples' shoes?

_____

_____

Don't be so independent or headstrong that you reject His help. You need the Lord, no matter how intelligent or strong you think you are.

The ways of the Lord are not our ways, and our abilities are nothing compared to His power. What does the Apostle Paul have to say about the worldly way of thinking? (Read 1 Corinthians 1:17-31.)

_____

_____

Continue to move self out the way and allow God to do a great work through you which benefits others.

-144-

Protector

Every word of God is pure: He is a shield unto them that put their trust in Him. (Proverbs 30:5 KJV)

You can trust the Lord to keep you safe from all hurt, harm, and danger. He has promised in His word, nothing deadly will harm you, nor can anyone come near you or destroy you.

Is there anything we should do to ensure God's protection will encircle us? In what way will He protect us from evil? (Read 2 Thessalonians 3:1-5.)

_____

_____

No weapons formed against you shall be able to prosper or succeed.

Read Isaiah 54:1-17.
What is the context of this passage? Who is it talking about?

_____

_____

Jesus is your Protector, He will shield, guard, and protect His people from all harm. Trust the Lord to keep you safe, secured, and wrapped in His loving arms. The Lord will always shield you, cause you to prosper, and you shall be kept alive.

God promised protection to the Israelites on what condition?
(Read Deuteronomy 30:9-10.)

_____

_____

You are protected from the storms, fiery darts, diseases, floods, winds, and any other manner of destruction trying to come against you.

-145-

No More Set-Backs

What shall we then say to these things? If God be
for us, who can be against us? (Romans 8:31 KN)

Who or what can come against God? Who, besides Him, is
OMNIPOTENT (All-powerful)? No one or nothing can stop
the move and plan of God. When those doors didn't open for
you, it was a delay—you were not denied.

God always gives us what we need, though it may not
always look the way we expect it to. What is some ways
God provided for you in unexpected ways?

_____

_____

This set-back was a set-up for God to thrust you into
your destiny and purpose. You will not look at a set-back
negatively or in the same way again. You were set-up for your
breakthrough. What you went through was only a test and a
learning experience.

Does testing come from the Devil or from God?
(James 1:2-4.)

_____

_____

Keep trusting, keep believing, keep praying, keep praising,
and keep receiving God's goodness. Your best is yet to come!
You are being set-up for greatness!

What exactly is the greatness that God has in store for His people?
(Read 2 Peter 1:2-4.)

_____

_____

Affirm that you desire to follow God, and that you truly want to obtain the reward He holds in store for those who follow Him. He will not withhold it from you!

-146-

In The Name Of Jesus

And whatsoever ye shall ask in My name, that will I do, that the Father may be glorified in the Son. If ye shall ask any thing in My name, I will do it. (John 14:13-14 KJV)

Be confident that your prayers are lining up with God's will. Whatever you ask in Jesus' name, He will do it. Keep developing, and drawing closer to God, and desiring a more intimate relationship with Him, through His Son, Jesus.

How can you ensure that what you want is in line with what Christ wants for you?
(Read Romans 12:2-23.)

_____

_____

God will grant your heart's desires. Continue to do what is pleasing in the sight of God and receive His promises, in the Name of Jesus.

What does it take to become pleasing to Jesus?
(Read Philippians 2:12-16.)

_____

_____

God delights in granting His children's most earnest requests.

What should we ask God for?
(Read 1 Peter 3:12-16.)

_____

_____

How can we know that God will hear our prayers?
(Read 1 John 5:14-15.)

_____

_____

Pray: *Lord, please align my will with Your own. Help me to desire only what I ought and grant my requests to follow and love you with my whole heart, soul, mind, and strength. Amen.*

-147-
Are You Ready?

Call unto Me, and I will answer thee, and shew thee great and mighty things, which thou knowest not. (Jeremiah 33:3 KJV)

Are you ready for the life-giving and life-changing Word? After accepting Jesus Christ as Lord and Savior, you are ready for Jesus to do a great work in you.

Ask Yourself...

Am I willing to accept the changes God's Word will bring to my life?

_____

_____

Will I be able to recognize the changes God completes in me?

_____

_____

Am I ready for the ultimate adventure of faith, or am I content with the status quo and the comfort of what I recognize and know?

_____

_____

God's Word is operating in you, through you, and for you. His Word can strengthen your inner man. He will change those things in your life which may need improvement.

Though it's probably well-known to you, **Read John 3:1-21**, focusing especially on the reason God sent Jesus to earth. Do you love the Light? How do you know?

_____

_____

Believe and receive by faith that everything that God has in store for you will come to fruition. Trust the Lord and watch Him do what only He can do. You are ready to do great and mighty things in the Kingdom of God.

-148-

My Past Is The Past

Remember ye not the former things, neither consider the things of old. Behold, I will do a new thing; now it shall spring forth; shall ye not know it? I will even make a way in the wilderness, and rivers in the desert. (Isaiah 43:18-19 KJV)

Your past is the past. Only visit the past when you are testifying about the goodness of God, how He delivered you and brought you from a mighty long way.

What is the imagery God uses to describe the "new thing" He is doing?
(Read Isaiah 43:16-21.)

_____

_____

Your life has been changed. It's not the same anymore, it's better. Do not let others bring up your past to disqualify you. The Lord has greater for you and your testimony is a steppingstone.

Name at least three things that God has delivered you from and explain how you have shown your gratitude to Him.

_____

_____

_____

_____

You are a living testimony, a miracle. You made it through the storms. You can look back and say, "Look where the Lord has brought me from."

Why does God take us through difficulties before He gives us rest and salvation?
(Read Psalm 66:8-12.)

_____

_____

_____

-149-

The Answer Is Found

For whatsoever things were written aforetime were written/or our learning, that we through patience and comfort of the scriptures might have hope. (Romans 15:4 KJV)

The Scriptures hold valuable lessons for all to heed. It teaches us about blessings and curses, right and wrong, good, and bad, righteousness and unrighteousness, obedience, and disobedience, born again and unsaved, Christians and unbelievers.

What does the Bible itself say about the purpose of the Scriptures?
(Read 2 Timothy 3:16.)

_____

_____

The Word of God is our roadmap and guide; we are to follow the instructions and directions in it. Everything we need is found in His Word. Nothing shall be added to His Word; neither shall anything be taken away from it.

What will happen to those who try to take away or add anything to the Word of God?
(Read Revelation 22:18-19.)

_____

_____

The Lord promised to comfort His people with His Word, and through the Scriptures give them hope. Read, study, and meditate on the Scriptures daily. You will find the answers you need.

If you haven't done so already, set aside time each day to read and study God's Word. Keep a journal and write down important things you learn. Try to read through the entire Bible in a year, and if that's too much, at least read a chapter each day.

-150-
Ignore Naysayers

A talebearer revealeth secrets: but he that is of a faithful spirit concealeth a matter. (Proverbs 11:13 KJV)

Do not allow naysayers to discourage and distract you. You may feel that you have no choice but to listen to what they're saying, but in fact, you can simply choose not to hear what they're speaking about or against you!

Naysayers may have their own agenda, and their own motivation for speaking against you. Do not focus on the negative things, but on the positive things.

Remember that those who speak against you may just be covering for their own insecurities. Try to think the best of them, and even try to speak good about them. You never know what might happen!

(Read Proverbs 25:21-22.)

_____

_____

Stay focused. Your efforts will eventually pay off. Keep doing what God has called and ordained for you to do. Your efforts and determination will be rewarded.

Trying to block out negative thoughts, seldomly, works as well as filling your mind with good thoughts. What does the Bible say about positive thoughts?

(Read Colossians 3:2 and Philippians 4:8.)

_____

Ignore negativity and press your way onto greater things in the Lord.

What does the Bible say about ignoring negativity spoken against you?
(Read Titus 3:10-11.)

_____

_____

Believe there are more people for you than against you.

Look Up

My voice shalt Thou hear in the morning, O LORD;
in the morning I will direct it unto Thee and will
look up. (Psalm 5:3 KJV)

Early in the morning, start looking up towards Heaven as you praise and direct your prayers to the Lord. Look up to see what is ahead and where you are going. Get into a habit of looking up.

What do the heavens themselves reveal to us? (Read Psalm 19:1.)

_____

_____

The Lord is waiting to reveal His plans to you. God has great things in store for you as you are obedient to His Word. While looking up, God is looking at you with a smile on His face.

When you look up into the sky, what do you see? Write at least three things, and what they tell you about God Himself.

_____

_____

He is delighted you chose to give Him honor and glory this morning. Keep looking up to receive divine help from the Lord.

Try writing your own psalm in praise of God's glory and the beauty of His creation. Read several of the Psalms of David for inspiration. It doesn't have to be perfect but do your best to tell God how you really feel. Then, go outside and read it to Him!

Look up and see the beauty of the day.
Read Ecclesiastes 3:9-13.
As you go through the rest of your day, write down everything you see that God has made beautiful in its time.

_____

_____

-152-

God Is Faithful

God is faithful, by whom ye were called unto the fellowship of His Son, Jesus Christ our Lord. (1 Corinthians 1:9 KJV)

God is faithful to His Word, for He cannot deny Himself. You can also be faithful for what you say and do.

Faithfulness Checklist:

What have you failed to be faithful in? Check all that apply, then commit to renewing your faithfulness in those things.

- ☐ Being a father or mother
- ☐ Being a son or daughter
- ☐ Telling others about your faith
- ☐ Being an employee or employer
- ☐ Paying your taxes
- ☐ Praying and reading your Bible every day

Especially when you commit to something, let your word be your bond. Be diligent and faithful in the things of God. Love on God. He is faithful and just to forgive your sins and to cleanse you from all unrighteousness.

Decree and Declare:

- ➤ *I will let my "yes" be "yes," and my "no" be "no"*
- ➤ *I will be diligent in everything God has given me to do*
- ➤ *I will love God with all my heart, soul, mind, and strength*

➤ *I will always repent of my sins and receive God's forgiveness in humility and gratitude.*

Always look forward to hearing the Lord say, "Well done, good and faithful servant, you have been faithful over a few things, I will make you ruler over many. "

-153-

A Willing Spirit

Watch and pray, that ye enter not into temptation: the spirit indeed is willing, but the flesh is weak.
(Matthew 26:41 KJV)

When we have a willing spirit, no one should force us to do anything. We shouldn't allow anyone or anything to get us off course.

Activate Your Power and Authority:

1. **Put your trust** wholly in God.
2. **Do not listen** to those who would distract us from the Christian way of life.
3. **Commit yourself** to God's will for your life.

Certainly, as mature Christians, we know right from wrong. Walking in the flesh causes people to go in a different direction which is contrary to the will of God. If we are not careful during those times, we may lose sight of what is important and pleasing to God. We may please others and our own flesh, but not please the Lord.

What does it look like to walk in the Spirit? What does it look like to walk in the flesh?
(Read Galatians 5:16-17.)

_____

_____

We must watch and pray and avoid worldly and fleshly temptations. It's important that we are walking by the Spirit. Therefore, we will not please our flesh, but desire to please the Lord. Pray, and have a willing heart to please God in your Christian walk.

Read Matthew 26:41.
How do we strengthen our flesh to resist temptation?

_____

_____

-154-

You Are Important

Wisdom is the principal thing; therefore, get wisdom: and with all thy getting get understanding. (Proverbs 4:7 KJV)

In this lifetime, each one of us may need to seek godly counsel from time to time. It's okay! Don't feel embarrassed to ask for help. NO one person knows it all.

What situations are you facing that you need advice about? Write down three things, and the name of one person you can talk to about each one:

1. _____
2. _____
3. _____

You are important to God. He wants you to seek Him for wisdom, knowledge, and understanding. God has delegated authorities when you need counsel, such as Pastors, Ministers, Leaders, Teachers, Mentors, and Professional Counselors.

What is your role in the Body of Christ? Who do you know that fills some of the other roles?
(Read 1 Corinthians 12:27-31.)

_____

_____

Don't try to figure everything out on your own. Pray and seek the Lord's face. Know Jesus loves you, and you are important to Him.

Read and reflect on Jeremiah 31:2-3.
Where has God taken you from? Where is He taking you?

_____

_____

-155-

Never Doubt

For verily I say unto you, That whosoever shall say unto this mountain, be thou removed, and be thou cast into the sea; and shall not doubt in his heart, but shall believe that those things which he saith shall come to pass; he shall have whatsoever he saith. (Mark 11:23 KJV)

Don't allow doubt to cause you to be afraid, or fear. Don't be confused to the point of not having any confidence in something, someone, or yourself. You can speak to those mountains great or small. Your mountain or obstacle may be debt, frustration, difficulties, hardships, mistakes, bad decisions, poor relationships, and the list could go on and on.

Mountain Checklist:

What mountains are in your way? How have you tried to deal with each one?

- ☐ Financial difficulties
- ☐ Family trouble
- ☐ Injury or illness
- ☐ Lack of faith or doubts
- ☐ Depression
- ☐ Fear of the unknown

These things are to be cast into the sea. When you cast them off, they cannot devour you. Pray and have confidence in the Lord. He will remove your mountain as you trust Him.

Never doubt. Believe in your heart that God has already provided everything you need.

Pray: *Dear God, deliver me from the things that seek to overcome me, and remind me daily of Your love for me and presence in my life. Remove the mountains and give me the strength for climbing. There is nothing You cannot do. I believe— help my unbelief.*

The Church

For if a man knows not how to rule his own house, how shall he take care of the church of God? (1 Timothy 3:5 KJV)

Since we do not like to neglect keeping our homes and office spaces clean, there should be no way we would fail in keeping the household of God in order.

One of the most famous incidents in the life of Christ is His cleansing of the Temple. **Read the story again** in John 2:13-17 and ask yourself if you have the same zeal for God's house. We may not need to drive out moneychangers, but what *does* need to be done in our places of worship to make them acceptable to God?

_____

_____

It takes each one of us doing something to contribute to the upkeep and cleanliness of our place of worship. We are servants of Christ: we should humble ourselves to clean the restrooms, dust, vacuum, sweep the floors, take out or pick up trash, clean windows, and glass doors, etc.

Church Maintenance Checklist:

Check off everything that needs to be done to your church building, and make sure someone is assigned to each task; if necessary, do it yourself!

- [ ] Landscape maintenance
- [ ] Fixing faulty plumbing
- [ ] Tidying up
- [ ] Cleaning
- [ ] Repainting (inside and outside)
- [ ] Fixing the roof
- [ ] Maintaining the parking lot

The heart of a servant will do what is needed to be done.

-157-

Victory

But thanks be to God, which giveth us the victory through our Lord Jesus Christ. (1 Corinthians 15:57 KJV)

You have victory over fear, doubt, misfortune, and disappointment.

Decree and Declare:

> ➤ *I will not be overcome by negative thoughts or emotions*

> ➤ *The Lord is my strength and my strong tower.*

> ➤ *Though I walk in the valley of the shadow of Death, I will fear no evil.*

> ➤ *Everything that weighs me down I will hand over to God.*

Incline your ears to hear what the Lord is saying. Cancel the other voices attempting to manipulate you, those things which try to keep you up at night. Start declaring you will sleep and rest in the Lord.

The Lord does not want His children to be deprived of sleep, which is necessary for our mental health and physical well-being. What is the secret to sleeping well? (Read Psalm 4:1-8.)

God has given you strength to fight against anything that comes your way. Trust in the Lord and know victory is yours!

What is the ultimate source of our strength?
(Read Isaiah 40:27-31.)

_____

_____

-158-
Come To God Rightfully

For He hath made Him to be sin for us, who knew
no sin; that we might be made the righteousness
of God in Him. (2 Corinthians 5:21 KJV)

We cannot expect to be blessed by God when we are intentionally disobedient. We must be in right standing with God, not doing things our own way, but doing things His way.

The Apostle Paul warns that in the last days disobedience will become common. What can we do to guard ourselves against it?
(Read 2 Timothy 3:1-9.)

_____

_____

When we come to God rightly, we receive all His blessings and benefits. It is only right and fitting as children of God that we do not waver at the things pertaining to the Kingdom of God. We must hunger and thirst after His righteousness.

What does it mean to hunger and thirst after righteousness?
(Read Matthew 5:6.)

_____

_____

_____

Be in right standing and be filled with His goodness.

Read Romans 5:1-21.
What is the source of our right standing with God?

_____

_____

Ask Yourself...

Do I really see myself as a child of God?

_____

_____

What does it mean to be a child of God?

_____

_____

159

Have No Fear

For God hath not given us the spirit of fear, but of power, and of love, and of a sound mind. (2 Timothy 1:7 KJV)

Cancel the thoughts and plans of the enemy. Have your mind made up that fear has no room in your life, but receive faith, power, love, peace, joy, and the goodness of the Lord.

What does the Apostle Paul say about fear? (2 Timothy 1:6-7.)

_____

_____

The enemy tries to keep God's people in bondage with fear. Some people fear the unknown because they don't know what today, tomorrow, or the future brings. Do not allow fear to rule and control your mind.

Decree and Declare:

➤ *Fear will not keep me from the love of God.*
➤ *I will not fear the future because I know and trust that God holds it in His hands.*
➤ *All my thoughts I turn over to Jesus, and He will rescue me from them, and from the fear they create.*
➤ *I will not fear the unknown, because all things are known to God, and I am His child.*

God has given you power and authority, even over your thoughts. Don't be afraid! He will deliver you from all your fears. Know without any doubt that fear doesn't control your life anymore because you have dominion over fear through the power of Jesus Christ.

160

Discern Both

But strong meat belongeth to them that are of full age, even those who by reason of use, have their senses exercised to discern both good and evil. (Hebrews 5:14 KJV)

Nothing shall be hidden from the Lord. The same shall be for the children of God who obey His Word.
What does this mean for you, personally?

_____

_____

The Lord will reveal the plan of the enemy to those who belong to Him. His children will be able to discern between good and evil.
What does it mean to discern between good and evil?

_____

_____

God's children will also have a spiritual awareness and understanding of His Word.
What is spiritual awareness? Do you, have it?

_____

_____

You must be spiritually mature to discern the things of God. Follow His righteousness and know God's ways are good.

What does it mean to be spiritually mature?

_____

_____

You shall not be deceived. The enemy's ways will always lead to destruction.

Read Proverbs 14:11-12.
What are the characteristics of the ways of man vs. the ways of God? How can you be sure you know the difference?

_____

_____

-161-

Those Who Follow

Then spake Jesus again unto them, saying, "I am the light of the world. He that followeth Me shall not walk in darkness but shall have the light of life." (Jesus in John 8:12 KJV)

Jesus is the Light of the world.

Read John 1:1-18.
What does it mean, "Jesus is the light of the world"?

_____

_____

Apart from Him, many will live in sin and darkness. Follow Jesus and give the invitation for others to know His marvelous light. There is no darkness which can overcome the light when we are in Christ.

What are the works of darkness?
(Read Romans 13:11-14.)

_____

_____

Believe in the Father and become children of the light.

What does it mean to be children of the light?
(Read 1 Thessalonians 5:1-11.)

_____

Every good and perfect gift comes from above, which also comes down from the Father of lights.
What does this mean?
(Read James 1:16-18.)

_____

_____

God is light, and in Him there is no darkness. Those who follow the Lord will have guidance, direction, protection, provision, and peace. Do not live life in darkness. Choose Jesus, He is the Light of life.

-162-

Glorify Him

The LORD is high above all nations and His glory above the heavens. (Psalm 113:4 KJV)

God, we reverence You! You are the Most Holy One! Oh Lord, we worship You in the beauty of holiness! Oh Lord, we send up the highest praise to You. Hallelujah!

What can you praise God for? Name as many things as you can think of, and then think of some more!

God, we honor your righteousness! Lord, we exalt, magnify, and glorify Your name above every name in heaven and earth!

What is the righteousness of God? Use an online concordance or Bible to find as many references as you can to God's righteousness in the Holy Scriptures.

Oh God, we give You thanks for sending Your Son, Jesus Christ. He is Lord and Savior, and through His blood our sins are washed away. Lord, we give You thanks. You are worthy of all our praise.

Ask Yourself...

Do I sometimes get tired of praising God? Why or why not?

What can I do to change that?

Is not praising God a form of idolatry?

-163-

Deal With It

And we know that all things work together for good to them that love God, to them who are the called according to His purpose. (Romans 8:28 KJV)

Many people have heard these sayings: "Learn to leave well enough alone," or "If it's not broken, why try to fix it?"

What do people mean by these phrases? Why might these not be good advice for one trying to lead the Christian life?

_____

_____

_____

We must deal with issues and matters before they get bigger. Do not put it off on someone else. Be proactive, and do not wait until things get out of control, or worse.

Proactive Checklist:

Which of these issues in your life is threatening to get out of control? What can you do to fix the problem before it gets worse?

- ☐ A disagreement with your spouse
- ☐ A child's resentment due to something you said or did
- ☐ Difficult relationships at work
- ☐ Sin you've kept hidden
- ☐ Out-of-control finances

☐ Too much time wasted
☐ Neglecting everyday duties or prayer

No matter how great or small the problem may appear, the Lord will fix it.

God does not want anyone to suffer more than necessary. He is always ready to intervene, but we must humble ourselves to receive His help. What is the single issue from the list above that most needs your attention? What will you do to make it right?

_____

_____

_____

-164-

You Made It Through

I went down to the bottoms of the mountains; the earth with her bars was about me forever: yet hast thou brought up my life from corruption, 0 LORD, my God. (Jonah 2:6 KJV)

Even though you were caught off guard when trouble came knocking at your door, it did not catch God by surprise. He knows what His children will face.

What biblical story shows us that God is not taken by surprise by anything that can happen to us?
(Read Psalm 95.)

_____

_____

He has strengthened you to go through the raging storms and dark valley experiences. God will give you the strength to stand up stronger than before.

Does the fact that God will give us strength mean that we will never face any difficulties? Why or why not?
(Read Psalm 91.)

_____

_____

Trust God while you're in the valley or in the pit. He will not leave you there. He is with you always. He will place you back on the mountain top.

Read Psalm 40.
What comfort do you draw from this chapter?

_____

_____

_____

Go ahead and shout! You will make it through.

Declare:

I will put my trust in the Lord, in whom is my salvation.

-165-

He Is Worthy

Thou art worthy, O Lord, to receive glory and honour and power: for Thou hast created all things, and for Thy pleasure they are and were created. (Revelation 4:11 KJV)

Jesus is worthy to be praised. We acknowledge, honor, exalt, glorify, magnify, and reverence His name. He is WORTHY! The Lord is worthy of all our worship and praise.

Why is the Lord worthy of praise?
(Read Psalm 86:12-13.)

_____

_____

Therefore, every knee shall bow, and every tongue shall confess that Jesus Christ is Lord.

Ironically, what is it that causes God the Father to praise our Lord Jesus Christ? How ought we to imitate this? (Read Philippians 2:1-11.)

_____

_____

Behold, He is the Lamb of God, who takes away the sins of the world. And worthy is the Lamb who was slain to receive power, riches, wisdom, strength, honor, glory, and blessings.

What about this can seem counterintuitive to a worldly way of thinking?

_____

_____

Let the people of God say, "Lord, we exalt Your name forever and ever. For You are Worthy to be praised. You are Worthy, no one can fathom Your greatness."

Sit quietly by yourself and contemplate God's greatness. Write down anything that comes to you.

_____

_____

-166-

God Supplies

But my God shall supply all your need according to His riches in glory by Christ Jesus. (Philippians 4:19 KJV)

The Lord is our Shepherd, and we shall not want.

Do you know which Psalm this is taken from? If not, try to find it in the Bible, and then commit it to memory. It is a great blessing to be able to recall God's words of promise to us!

Our Heavenly Father continues to supply us with everything we need. When we are devoted and faithful, the Lord will always supply our needs. The Lord's supply is never lacking. We don't need to worry about water, food, shelter, clothing, money, or anything needed to survive.

Read Matthew 6:25-34 again.
Think what this passage means in terms of God being our Father. Do you really believe that? If so, how should that affect the way you live?

_____

_____

You will never suffer lack, for there is no want to them that fear the Lord. The Lord will always make provision for His people. He has promised in His word.

Read Psalm 34:8-10.

Ask Yourself...

Do I really trust God to provide even the small things?

_____

_____

Does my worry get in the way of my needs being filled?

_____

_____

Have I ever not had my basic needs met?

_____

_____

-167-

Look To God

I will lift up mine eyes unto the hills, from whence cometh my help. My help cometh from the LORD which made heaven and earth. (Psalm 121:1-2 KJV)

In life you may be able to overlook other people, but your life is in danger if you choose to overlook God.

Ask Yourself...

Who have I overlooked, and how can I truly see them?

_____

_____

Have I overlooked God? Why or why not?

_____

_____

What practical things can I do to keep myself from overlooking other people in the future?

_____

_____

What practical things can I do to keep myself from overlooking God in the future?

_____

You should look to God. He is your source for everything you want and need to survive. Look to God for strength, directions, instructions, and for guidance, you will not go wrong. He has your life in His hands. He is willing and waiting for you to look to Him. The Lord is your Helper! Look to Him for inspiration, encouragement, strength, power, faith, confidence, love, joy, peace, answers, comfort, guidance, wisdom, knowledge, understanding, blessings, favor, provision, and His promises. Look to the Lord in everything and for all things.

Declare:

I will no longer overlook You, Lord. Help me to keep my eyes on You!

-168-

Through This Experience

Thou will keep him in perfect peace; whose mind is stayed on thee; because he trusteth in thee. Trust ye in the LORD for ever; for in the LORD JE-HO-VAH is everlasting strength. (Isaiah 26:3-4 KJV)

The trials, situations, or circumstances you had to endure are over! You made it out. Yes, it was tough, and you had to hold on to your faith with all your, might but the good news is you did not give up. You stood the test.

Look back on a time in your life that you endured great difficulty through your faith in God. How did He strengthen you? What did you do to keep your eyes on Him?

This life experience strengthened you, and you saw God's hand in it. You realized, even though you were going through the rain, flood, storm, fire, and draught, you still had the peace of God. Always trust and depend on the Lord.

Commit to God that you will always call on Him in all of life's difficulties, that you will not blame Him for trials, and that you will even thank Him for the rough times which He uses for your good.

What specifically will you do to keep this commitment? He will make a way and bring you through it all.

_____

_____

Pray: *I cannot make it through any of life's difficulties by myself, Lord. Help me to always look to you for strength and guidance, and do not let me become embittered when I encounter strengthening experiences. Amen.*

The Reality Is

For with God nothing shall be impossible.
(Luke 1:37 KJV)

The reality is that nothing shall be impossible for you. There are more resources and opportunities made available for the advancement of God's people than you can imagine. You can attain a higher education, a better paying job, a bigger promotion, or even start your own business, or travel around the world.

What are your ambitions? Write them down, and then check to see if they align with God's will for your life.

_____

_____

You can advance to the top because nothing is unreachable or impossible with God. Set your mind on the goals you are trying to attain, and work hard, knowing that success comes only from the Lord.

What will you do *today* to start reaching your goals?

_____

_____

Diligently work and seek Him during, the waiting. Pray, believe, and receive your breakthrough.

Declare:

> ➤ *On my own I can do nothing, but through Christ I can do all things because He strengthens me.*
> ➤ *I will wait patiently, knowing that God works all things to the good of those who love Him.*
> ➤ *Today I will make a new beginning, knowing that Christ Himself makes all things new.*

-170-

Let Them See

I am crucified with Christ: nevertheless I live; yet not I, but Christ liveth in me: and the life which I now live in the flesh I live by the faith of the Son of God, who loved me, and gave Himself for me. (Galatians 2:20 KJV)

Let the people see Jesus in your love walk and in your conversations. Let the people see Jesus in your personality and in your character. Let them see that you have the heart of Jesus as you serve others.

Be honest with yourself and record what people see when they look at you.

_____

_____

Let other people see God's power and anointing operating in your life. When others look upon you, will they see the grace of God in your life?

Pray: *Lord, grant that others will see You in me. Christ in the heart of all who think of me, Christ in the mouth of all who speak of me, Christ in the eyes of all who see me, Christ in the ears of all who hear me.*

Walk as Christians, being filled with God's strength, faith, joy, peace, goodness, righteousness, meekness, holiness, and lovingkindness. Let the people see, Christ who lives in you, the hope of glory.

Can you name the Fruits of the Spirit from memory? **Read** Galatians 5:22-23.

_____

_____

Check your work. How many did you get right? How many of these do you still need to work on?

-171-
Serenade The Lord

I will sing of the mercies of the LORD forever: with my mouth I make known thy faithfulness to all generations. (Psalm 89:1 KJV)

Make a joyful noise unto the Lord! Serve Him with gladness and come into His presence with singing. Why not sing unto the Lord a sweet love song?

Go ahead, **sing your favorite hymn or praise song to God!** If you can play an instrument, accompany yourself.

Serenade the Lord just because of His goodness and lovingkindness. Sing spiritual songs with thanksgiving in your heart. Serenade the Lord and experience His love and tranquility.

Read Ephesians 5:17-21.
Why do you think the Apostle Paul gives, these instructions to the church in Ephesus? If necessary, read the rest of the Epistle for context.

_____

_____

In your time of praise and worship, sing to the Lord a new song. Sing a sweet melody to the Lord because of His love for you.

Make a habit of singing your praises to God. Try starting every morning with a song, and sing throughout the day as you are able. It might seem unnatural at first, but soon you won't be able to keep yourself from praising the Lord! Do this for an entire week, and then write a reflection about what you learned, how you felt, and how it helped you.

_____

_____

_____

_____

-172-

God Promises

For all the promises of God in Him are Yea, and in Him Amen, unto the glory of God by us. (2 Corinthians 1:20 KJV)

We have all the promises of God through Jesus Christ.

The Scriptures are full of God's promises. Find a few, and write them here, along with the reference so you can find them again. Think about how they apply to you.

_____

_____

He is so faithful to fulfil all His promises. His promises cannot fail because of His nature.
What is the nature of God?

_____

_____

God promised to provide for those who trust and believe in Him. The Lord has graciously made His declarations to His people through His Word. He will not go back on His promises.
What does it mean that God will not go back on His promises?

_____

_____

God's Word is absolute. Every promise God made has been fulfilled, and not one promise has failed. God's promises are made available to all who will believe and receive.

Think about the promises you've made and failed to keep. What happened as a result?

_____

_____

What prevented you from keeping your promise? Did you clearly communicate to those you made your promise to that you would not be able to keep the commitment? If not, how would things have gone if you had?

_____

_____

_____

-173-

Keep Pushing

Knowing this, that the trying of your faith worketh patience. But let patience have her perfect work, that ye may be perfect and entire, wanting nothing. (James 1:3-4 KJV)

When situations occur or problems arise, don't grumble give it to Jesus. Put your faith and trust in the Lord. Allow Him to work it out. The Lord will embrace and strengthen you through this trial.

ReRead Philippians 2:14-16.
How does complaining affect our circumstances? How does it (or how doesn't it) help us to persevere? How does it affect our relationship with God?

_____

_____

Keep pushing, keep praising Him and activating your faith. Don't become impatient. Push harder. Your breakthrough is coming. You can't stop now. You are so close. Your breakthrough is just in arm's reach.

Read Hebrews 12:1.
How does thinking about our life trials as an athletic competition help us to persevere?

_____

_____

Keep pushing. Know there isn't anything your Heavenly Father wouldn't do for His own. While you are in the waiting process, keep pushing. You are going to walk in everything God has called for you to walk in.

Read Psalm 25:10.
Do you believe what the Psalmist says? Why or why not?

_____

_____

-174-

Make an Impact

Let your light so shine before men, that they may see your good works, and glorify your Father which is in heaven. (Matthew 5:16 KJV)

Have you impacted any lives that you know of, or vice versa? Let your light shine bright at all times. Allow your light to consume the darkness that others are walking in. When they encounter the presence of God that's in you, darkness will leave them immediately.

Evaluate your frequent friends and companions (but do not judge them!). Are they causing you to walk in the light, or the darkness? Are you able to maintain your Christian witness when you spend all your time with ungodly people?

_____

_____

_____

_____

You are a person with good character and great influence, people are watching you even when you are not aware of it. It's very important that you conduct yourself respectfully and humbly.

_____

_____

God created humanity to live together. It is only natural that we are all people of influence. Do others see Christ in you?

_____

_____

_____

Thank God, you have positive role models surrounding you every day. You can make an impact in the lives of others by encouraging them to be the best, man, woman, boy, or girl that God has called them to be.
Who are the role models in your life? Do you regularly follow their advice, or just persist in what you were already doing?

_____

_____

Make a spiritual impact in the lives of others.
What is one practical way you can do this today?

_____

_____

-175-

Good Success

This book of the law shall not depart out of thy mouth; but thou shalt meditate therein day and night, that thou mayest observe to do according to all that is written therein: for then thou shalt make thy way prosperous, and then thou shalt have good success. (Joshua 1:8 KJV)

You are on your way to good success as you apply godly principles to your life daily. Watch God perfect greatness in you. He has already placed everything inside of you, to bring forth His plan and will for your life.

What did Jesus say about the location of the Kingdom of God?

(Read Luke 17:20-21.)

_____

_____

He wants to expand and stretch you greater and farther than what your finite mind can comprehend. He knows you are trustworthy and can be trusted with good success and riches.

What are the riches that God wants to entrust you with?

(Read Ephesians 3:14-19.)

_____

_____

Commit your works unto the Lord, your plans will succeed. Continue soaring in the Kingdom of God. You are a winner. You are victorious.

Ask Yourself...

Do I live as though Christ is within me?

_____

_____

What would it look like if I did?

_____

_____

Are there any people in my life that live as though Christ is in them?

_____

_____

What do their lives look like?

_____

_____

-176-

Power Produced

And behold, I send the promise of My Father upon you: but tarry ye in the city of Jerusalem, until ye be endued with power from on high. (Luke 24:49 KJV)

The more you seek God and meditate on His Word, you are empowered. Staying in the presence of God in worship produces power. Praying and fasting empowers you to hear from God.

When Moses met God on Mt. Sinai, he prepared himself to encounter God by fasting. Have you ever tried this? How did it help you to discern the voice of God?

_____

_____

Studying the Scriptures and applying them to your life daily will produce power. If you don't have the Spirit of God dwelling within you, you can acquire Him by accepting Jesus Christ as your Lord and Savior.

Whether or not you have ever asked Jesus into your heart, **do so now**. Ask Him to fill you with His love and mercy, to forgive your sins, and to show you all the ways you should go. Do not be ashamed of anything you have done but confess everything to God so that He may forgive all your sins. Do not leave it at that—pray to Jesus Christ every day, and day-by-day, renew your relationship with Him through prayer and Bible reading.

Press in—you shall receive power after the Holy Spirit has come upon you. The Holy Spirit will empower, strengthen, and equip you to do the work God has called for your life.

What has God called you to do? Have you done it?

_____

_____

Embrace the grace of God which will come upon you and empower you to do what you could not achieve or accomplish in your own strength.

Pray: *Lord, grant me your grace. I know You love me, and desire me to walk in Your ways. Help me to walk in power. In the name of Jesus, Amen.*

-177-

Stop Holding onto It

But as for you, ye thought evil against me; but God meant it unto good to bring to pass, as it is this day, to save much people alive. (Genesis 50:20 KJV)

I say to you today: stop holding onto insecurities, hurt, baggage, rejection, disappointment. Sometimes you may have to face these difficult things, but you do not have to allow these things to linger on.

Insecurities Checklist:

What insecurities are you harboring that keep you from reaching your full potential in Christ? Are you insecure about:

- ☐ Your appearance
- ☐ Your career or wages
- ☐ Your lack of knowledge or education
- ☐ Your shortcomings as a child, parent, or friend
- ☐ Fear of the future
- ☐ Fear of the past catching up with you

If someone did you wrong, mistreated you, or lied to you, forgive them, and move forward. Right now, you need to release it and let it go.

Is there any limit to how much we should forgive others? (Read Matthew 18:21-35.)

_____

_____

Jesus knows all about your trials. He can turn your situation around. Have faith, and believe things are getting better in your life right now.

Think of one person you need to forgive. Forgive them in your heart, and then try to reconcile with them. Record what happens.

178

Keep On Going

Brethren, I count not myself to have apprehended: but this one thing I do, forgetting those things which are behind, and reaching forth unto those things which are before. I press toward the mark for the prize of the high calling of God in Christ Jesus. (Philippians 3:13-14 KJV)

You cannot quit now! You have come too far to turn back. You may get a little fatigued at times, but keep on pressing toward the prize, JESUS.

Sometimes you need to put a little space between you and the world in order to gain the strength to keep going. Set aside some time to spend with God, just you and Him. Pray and read your Bible and write down anything that comes to you.

_____

_____

_____

_____

The more you acknowledge Christ and call on His name, the better you will feel, and the more you will be empowered for the journey, no matter what is going on all around you. The Lord will give you saving grace.

Sometimes it can be helpful to remember a time God gave you strength you didn't know you had to carry on. Remember such a time and write it down. Come back to it when you're feeling low.

_____

_____

_____

_____

Continue to be encouraged and pray for guidance and strength to keep moving forward. Stay focused. Keep pressing ahead. Keep going.

You'll never get where you're going if you stop thinking about your goal. Write down the main thing you're striving for right now and keep it in mind as you go about your day.

_____

_____

Allow the Holy Spirit to lead and guide you.

179

Speak the Truth

Sanctify them through Thy truth: Thy word is truth. (John 17:17 KJV)

When you uphold the Word of God, you are speaking truth. God's Word is true, and the truth will set you free.
What is God's Word?

_____

_____

Demonstrate God's love and truth to those with whom you come in contact. Believers don't get caught up in lying, telling fables, and spreading rumors about others which are not true.
Our words have consequences. What is one way you can keep yourself from speaking, things that aren't true?

_____

_____

Share God's truth with those you know, and with those you don't know. When you speak God's Word, many people around the world will be impacted. Their lives will be changed for the better.
How can words you speak affect people all over the world? How does this make you think about the importance of what you say?

_____

_____

Speak God's truth as you read and study His Word, from Genesis to Revelation.

If you haven't already, **commit** to reading the entire Bible this year. Journal as you go, writing down everything that strikes you, or things God lays on your heart or reveals to you. Download an app to help you keep track, and to hold you accountable!

Ask Yourself...

What do I do to encourage others to read the Scriptures?

_____

_____

180

What Have You Lost?

And the LORD turned the captivity of Job, when he prayed for his friends; also the LORD gave Job twice as much as he had before. (Job 42:10 KJV)

Jesus Christ is a Restorer. He will restore everything stolen or taken from you. This is good news for the people of God. You haven't lost anything. The Lord will restore those things back to you again.

What are the things that God will restore to you?
(Read Deuteronomy 30:1-20.)

_____

_____

God is looking to give you double for your troubles. Keep trusting in His Word. The Lord is going to restore everything you have lost, and more.

Do ask God for restoration?
(Read Psalm 51:10-12.)

_____

_____

The Lord will give you a double portion of His love, joy, peace, grace, mercy, strength, healing, anointing, goodness, wealth, and prosperity.

Decree and Declare:

➤ *I will trust God for all good things.*

➤ *There is nothing in this world that can prevent God from restoring to me His mercy and compassion.*

➤ *I will desire the things of God, not the things of flesh.*

➤ *I will not worry about what I don't have. I will wait to receive from Him what He has in store for me.*

-181-

A Father Who Cares

Casting all your care upon Him, for He careth for you. (1 Peter 5:7 KJV)

Just like a father who cares for his sons and daughters in the natural your Heavenly Father cares even more for His children.

Have you taken the time to ask God for what you need? Write these things down and ask God for them when you go to Him in prayer. Record in your journal what happens.

_____

_____

_____

He cares deeply about your personal relationship with Him. He is concerned about you. He cares about your spiritual walk, physical well-being, and your financial growth. Abba (Father) is concerned about your family, friends, jobs, health, and future.

Do you care about these things as much as God does? What does this mean for your relationship with Him, and with them?

_____

_____

_____

If you have any problems, cast all your burdens on the Lord and leave them there. God wants to see His children happy, healthy, whole, and enjoying life abundantly.

Do you enjoy life? What changes do you need to make in order to do so?

_____

_____

_____

It's time for you to be free from those things troubling you. Cast all your cares upon the Lord, for He cares for you.

Pray: *Lord, take from me everything that comes between me and true peace and happiness. Show me what to do, and how to do it, and keep me walking on the pathway that leads to Life. Do not let me fall.*

A Clean Temple

What? know ye not that your body is the temple of the Holy Ghost, which is in you, which ye have of God, and ye are not your own? For ye are bought with a price: therefore glorify God in your body, and in your spirit, which are God's. (1 Corinthians 6:19:20 KJV)

It's imperative that God's people have clean hands and pure hearts. The Holy Spirit is looking for clean temples to dwell in.

Read 1 Corinthians 6:19-20.
What does it mean that "you are not your own"?

_____

_____

Make sure that your business is in order. Instead of finding fault, judging, and being overly critical towards others, look at yourself.
When you look inside, what do you see?
(Read Luke 6:41-42.)

_____

_____

Cherish your body in a godly fashion. Be mindful of what you put in your body. It's time for you to break the bad habits.
What bad habits do you need to put aside? Overeating, smoking, drinking too much, not exercising, all these can

affect our ability to do the work of God. Choose one from your list and make steps today to give it up.

_____

_____

God doesn't want His people carrying any unforgiveness, strife, malice, bitterness, or hurt in their heart. Let us continue to pray. The Lord will remove everything trying to hinder, contaminate, or destroy the destiny of His people.

-183-

Vision Is Needed

Where there is no vision, the people perish, but he that keepeth the law, happy is he. (Proverbs 29:18 KJV)

You must activate the Word of God by faith. the Word works if you take full advantage of it and apply it consistently. You need the Word of God for revelation, and to see change. Without revelation, you will stay in bondage and have no power. What is the meaning of revelation?

_____

_____

You are truly blessed when you honor and keep God's Word alive in your heart. You must spend quality time in prayer, praise, worship, and in studying His Word.

Ask Yourself...

How do I keep God's Word alive in my heart?

_____

_____

How much time do I actually spend in worship and Bible study each day?

_____

_____

Am I familiar with God's Word, or does it seem foreign to me?

_____

_____

Do I have someone to teach and explain to me what, I don't understand?

_____

_____

God's Word will love you, keep you, protect you, correct you, strengthen you, provide for you, guide you, instruct you, teach you, encourage you, comfort you, and sustain you.

Declare:

> ➤ *I know that all my hope, strength, and comfort comes from the Lord, because His Word tells me so.*

-184-

Be Joyful

But let all those that put their trust in Thee rejoice: let them ever shout for joy, because Thou defendest them: let them also that love Thy name be joyful in Thee. (Psalm 5:11 KJV)

To know you made it through another day, month, or year is enough to rejoice! Rejoice when you see the Lord using your children, relatives, friends, co-workers, or a stranger.

It is not enough just to thank God for what He has done for you. Give thanks for what He has done for others, as well!

Write down the names of at least five people God is using and thank Him for each of them! Find a way to encourage each one, and then do so.

Whatever, you ask in the name of Jesus, be joyful. Know, with great consolation, that your joy is complete in Him.

What is joy? Is it the same as happiness?

Relax, rest, and be filled with the joy of the Lord. Be joyful and live a blessed life in the Lord.

Every day with God is a blessing, no matter what may be happening around us or to us. How can you tap into that blessing, even during difficult situations?

_____

_____

Know that you are blessed, that you can experience His unspeakable joy.

Have you ever experienced unspeakable joy in the Lord? What was it like, and when did it come to you?

-185-

The Comforter

Blessed be God, even the Father of our Lord Jesus Christ, the Father of mercies, and the God of all comfort; Who comforteth us in all our tribulation, that we may be able to comfort them which are in any trouble, by the comfort wherewith we ourselves are comforted of God. (2 Corinthians 1:3-4 KJV)

Please do not worry or fret. The Spirit of the Lord will not leave you comfortless. THE COMFORTER will comfort you through any pain, despair, difficulty, or affliction.
Name the pain, despair, and affliction in your life right now:

_____

_____

In Him, you will find comfort, consolation, and compassion.
Name the comfort, consolation, and compassion you are waiting to experience in the Lord:

_____

_____

THE COMFORTER has come to give you rest. Be thankful and grateful unto God for giving you a HELPER!
How does the Holy Spirit help us in our daily lives?

_____

_____

The Holy Spirit shall abide with you forever.

"Forever" is a big idea. What comes to mind when you think about it?

_____

_____

This is good news! THE COMFORTER, the Holy Spirit, will lead, guide, teach, counsel, and bring things back to your remembrance.

What have you forgotten? Ask God to help you remember, and write it here:

_____

_____

_____

-186-

The Gospel of Peace

And your feet shod with the preparation of the gospel of peace. (Ephesians 6:15 KJV)

Daily, be ready to share the Gospel of peace. With every step you take, walk in love, peace, and power. Be ready to share and spread the Gospel of peace to all men.

In order to be able to share the Gospel with everyone, you must know it inside and out. How well do you know the Gospel? What is the Gospel? Are you always on the lookout for ways to introduce others to it?

_____

_____

_____

_____

_____

Continue to seek peace, pursue it, and let the peace of God abide in your heart. Allow God's peace to continuously be multiplied in your life. The Lord is the Prince of Peace. He will give you peace at all times and in all areas of your life.

What is peace? What would it look like for peace to be present in every area of your life?

_____

_____

Follow the beautiful feet of Jesus and partake of His everlasting peace. God's word declares, "Blessed are the peacemakers, for they shall be called the children of God."

Can you list the rest of the Beatitudes? **Read** Matthew 5:3-12 and see which ones you've forgotten. Write them here and try to explain each one with just a few words.

_____

_____

_____

_____

_____

-187-

God Multiplies

Now He that ministereth seed to the sower both minister bread for your food, and multiply your seed sown, and increase the fruits of your righteousness. (2 Corinthians 9:10 KJV)

The Lord sees you sowing seeds into good and fertile ground.

Read Mark 4:1-20.
Are you sowing enough seeds to ensure some of them are falling on fertile ground? How can, you be sure?

_____

_____

He sees you being faithful in your giving. He saw how you stepped out in faith, sowing your best seed. Your seeds have been planted and watered, and God will give the increase.
Where do our seeds come from? What do we mean when we call them "seeds"?
God will increase your ability to give. God will continue to multiply your seeds greatly.

Read Luke 6:38.
Ironically, how can you get more seeds?

_____

_____

Start declaring that there is abundance, plenty, increase, more than enough, and divine overflow coming your way. He will also multiply to you more of His grace, mercy, righteousness, power, anointing, faith, meekness, and favor.

Decree and Declare:

> ➤ *I will give all I have in the power of God.*

> ➤ *I will patiently await God's increase, replenishing all that I have given from my great abundance.*

-188-

Be Determined

Now our Lord Jesus Christ Himself, and God, even our Father, which hath loved us, and hath given us everlasting consolation and good hope through grace. Comfort your hearts and stablish you in every good word and work. (2 Thessalonians 2:16-17 KJV)

The Lord has given His children strength and courage to move forward in this race we call life. Be determined even the more to spend intimate and quality time in the presence of the Lord. Diligently operate and oversee the things pertaining to kingdom work.

What kingdom work are you currently engaged in? What kingdom work would you *like* to be involved in? Do you need to let anything go in order to take on what God is calling you to? Write a short plan for how you will serve the Kingdom.

_____

_____

_____

_____

_____

Be determined to live a healthier life and lifestyle before the Lord. Have a positive outlook on life and the tenacity to do good and mighty things in the earth.

Healthy thoughts lead to a healthy body, and a healthy body is needed to do the work God has set aside for us. How can you improve your health in order to stay active in the Kingdom?

_____

_____

_____

_____

Be determined to stay in the will of God. He will advance and promote you in due time. Be determined to go beyond the norms. Go for God's best. You are STRONG! You are BLESSED! You are COURAGEOUS! You are a WINNER! You are VICTORIOUS!

-189-

My Help

I will lift up mine eyes unto the hills, from whence cometh my help. My help cometh from the LORD, which made heaven and earth. (Psalm 121:1-2 KJV)

Take the time to acknowledge that your help comes from the Lord who made heaven and earth. This help is divine and comes from our Father above.

Read Psalm 121:1-8.
Reflect on what this chapter means for you, right now.

_____

_____

_____

_____

The Lord is your Helper. He is here to assist and help you with whatever you're needing. The LORD is your Helper, Keeper, Sustainer, Protector, and Provider.

Pray that God will help you, keep you, sustain you, protect you, and provide for your needs.

Write down how He answers your prayer.

_____

_____

He is always leading, guiding, supporting, assisting, upholding, and guarding the hearts of His people. Call on Jesus and watch how quickly your Helper shows up.

Can you discern how Christ is currently guiding and assisting you? Are you open to His leading? What obstacles are preventing you from following Him? Have you asked Him to remove them?

_____

_____

_____

_____

_____

-190-

Opportunity

As we have therefore opportunity, let us do good unto all men, especially unto them who are of the household of faith. (Galatians 6:10 KJV)

Whenever you have an opportunity to be a blessing to someone, do it. Don't limit the kindness God has placed on the inside of you.

> **Read** 2 Corinthians 9:6-7.
> Who has God put on your heart to serve?

_____

_____

You have the heart to constantly give, and it's not out of obligation, nor is it to be seen or acknowledged. You have a sincere heart, and being a giver brings you joy. Cheerfully, you love blessing your Pastors and Leaders. They are praying and watching over your souls.

> **Read** 1 Timothy 5:17-18.
> Do you give regularly to your church? Do you tithe? Come up with a plan for giving and write it here.

_____

_____

You love to bless your children because they are yours. There are so many opportunities for giving! You can be a blessing in the schools, nursing homes, churches, and charities. Don't miss your opportunity to give, serve, and to be a blessing.

There are so many people around you in need. Choose one individual or organization, and plan to give to them in some way. It doesn't have to be money: you can give your time, your talent, your treasure, or even just give a good word. Write down what happens after you've given from your abundance.

_____

_____

_____

_____

-191-

See Yourself Prosperous

And he shall be like a tree planted by the rivers of water, that bringeth forth his fruit in his season, his leaf shall not wither and whatsoever he doeth shall prosper. (Psalm 1:3 KJV)

Start seeing yourself prospering in every area of your life. Continue to stay rooted and grounded in the things of God. Daily, walk in love, and carry out God's purpose, plan, and will for your life. You shall receive the blessings and promises of God because you did it His way.

Try to imagine what your life would like if you were truly prospering in the things of God. How can you get there?

_____

_____

_____

Don't be easily moved or persuaded by people who are not being led by God. Stay focused on God. He has prepared great things for you. Do what the Lord has required of you. Do what is right and good in the sight of the Lord. You will prosper in all you do and wherever you go.

Are there any people close to you who are not being led by God? What can you do to help them restructure their lives? Have you offered them up to God in prayer?

_____

_____

Keep living a healthy lifestyle and obeying God's Word. You will prosper, increase, and bear much fruit.

What kind of health will come to you when you obey God's Word? What kind of fruit might you bear?

Pray: *Lord Jesus, make a firm foundation for me. Do not let me be swayed by those who would distract me from You.*

Enjoy What You Have

Better is the sight of the eyes than the wandering of desire: this is also vanity and vexation of spirit.
(Ecclesiastes 6:9 KJV)

God's commandments warn us not to covet our neighbor's house. We must enjoy what God has given us and be content. Don't try to keep up with "the Joneses" attaining material goods. It comes, and it goes.

Read Exodus 20:17 and Matthew 6:19-21.
What attitude should we have towards possessions? How can we cultivate this in our lives when we live in such a materialistic culture that places great importance on what we own?

_____

_____

_____

_____

Sometimes, when you get the things, you saw your neighbor with, it doesn't give you the satisfaction you thought it would. Look to the Lord and enjoy what you have.

Ask Yourself...

Do I love things more than I should?

_____

Am I truly content, or do I harbor a desire for more in my heart?

_____

_____

Am I generous with what I have, or do I keep it all for myself?

_____

_____

Only desire what's in your heart. Learn to be satisfied or content. Enjoy what God has given you and be happy for your neighbors.

-193-

Still Standing

So shall they fear the name of the LORD from the west, and His glory from the rising of the sun. When the enemy comes in like a flood, the Spirit of the LORD shall ltft up a standard against him.
(Isaiah 59:19 KJV)

Life's circumstances tried to destroy you. However, you are still standing, by the grace of God. Take a praise break right here. HALLELUJAH! THANK YOU, JESUS! You thought you couldn't cope with the troubles you were facing, but you did.

Why does God allow difficult times in our life?
(Read Hebrews 12:11.)

_____

_____

The enemy took his best shot at you, but, thanks be unto God, you are still standing. You decided to stand firmly on the word of the Lord and call on His holy name.
Are you vigilant for attacks from the enemy?
(Read 1 Peter 5:8-9.)

_____

_____

You have acknowledged God as your Father, Lord, Savior, Protector, Deliverer, and Redeemer. He has given you peace

372 — LUVERTA HOOD BOULWARE

right in the midst of your storm. Oh, what a MIGHTY GOD you serve.

Decree and Declare:

> ➤ *God is my refuge and fortress, and I will hope in Him!*

> ➤ *God is my source of peace, and I will not look for it in anything or from anyone else.*

> ➤ *No matter what storms seek to wash away my foundation, I will stand secure, for it is Christ who strengthens me.*

> ➤ *I will praise my God all the day long, for He has rescued me out of the pit.*

Until I See My Savior

Ye shall walk after the LORD your God, and fear Him, and keep His commandments, and obey His voice, and ye shall serve Him, and cleave unto Him. (Deuteronomy 13:4 KJV)

Do not go after other gods and follow false prophets. These individuals or groups may tempt God's people to practice idolatry. They will lead you astray from God's truth.

Idol Checklist:

Which of these do you seek comfort from, instead of resting only in God's love?

- ☐ Possessions
- ☐ Spouse
- ☐ Social status
- ☐ Sexual relationships
- ☐ Pornography
- ☐ Your physical health and appearance

Commit today that you will fervently call on God to deliver, you from any of the idols that you checked on the above list.

We may not bow down to our idols nowadays, but they are all around us. How can you recognize what is an idol, and guard yourself against its seductiveness?

Make a declaration that you will serve the True and Living God until you die. Listen to God's voice, and only do what He commands you to do. Cling to the Lord wholeheartedly.

Desire to obey His word forever. Desire to serve the Lord until you see your Savior face to face.

How can you listen to God's voice?

_____

_____

-195-

Sitting at His Feet

And she had a sister called Mary, which also sat at Jesus feet, and heard His word. But Martha was cumbered about much serving, and came to Him, and said, Lord, dost Thou not care that my sister hath left me to serve alone? Bid her therefore that she help me. (Luke 10:39-40 KJV)

Sitting at the feet of Jesus is honoring God.

How is this honoring God? Explain as simply as you can.

_____

_____

When listening carefully, you can hear Jesus exalting the Father in His teachings. Don't allow yourself to be distracted to the point of missing the Lord's teachings, instructions, directions, and counsel.

What distracts you from hearing the voice of Christ? Are your distractions things you can remove from your life entirely, or are they things that simply have to be given their proper place? Why or why not?

_____

_____

_____

_____

Enter a place of humility, where you worship Christ in adoration. There is rest for your soul sitting at the feet of Jesus; take the time to sit there. Leave all your burdens at His feet.

What is humility? How can you attain it?

_____

_____

_____

God's amazing grace will humble you!

As you go about your day, practice giving all the space to the other person, seeking to imitate the humility of Jesus. Write down what happens when you do so, and how you reacted.

_____

_____

_____

-196-

The Pressing

For He had healed many; insomuch that they pressed upon Him for to touch Him, as many as had plagues. (Mark 3:10 KJV)

The people pressed upon Jesus. They needed a touch from Him.

What did the people expect to get just from touching Jesus?

_____

_____

Have you ever been pressed on every side? Have you ever felt crushed in your spirit, or felt empty inside?

Think back to a time you felt this way. What did you do, and what lifted you out of your slump?

_____

_____

_____

_____

If you can relate, I encourage you to keep pressing, you need a touch from the Lord.

Read Luke 8:43-48.

What does this story mean for us today? How can we touch Jesus, even though He isn't physically walking among us?

_____

Have faith in God. Get in His presence. Seek His face for a release. Desire a spiritual, financial, physical, mental, and emotional touch. One touch from the LORD will change the trajectory of your life forever.

Pray: *Lord, one touch from You is all I need. Do not let my pride, my sinfulness, or my lack of faith get in the way of feeling Your touch. Every time I try to fix my problems on my own, they end up worse than before. Empower me to lay myself aside, and to allow You to bring peace and order in my life. Help me to walk in Your ways, and always to give You all the gratitude and thanksgiving.*

-197-

How Powerful You Are

For though He was crucified through weakness, yet He liveth by the power of God. For we also are weak in Him, but we shall live with Him by the power of God toward you. (2 Corinthians 13:4 KJV)

It's very important that you remain connected to the greatest power source. God is OMNIPOTENT, He is All-Powerful. What does it mean that God is all-powerful?

_____

_____

_____

It's important that you worship where the Word of God is being taught, and that the Pastors and church members are operating with power.

What happens when you worship in a place where the Word of God is not taught, or where the shepherds of the flock are not operating in the power of the Most High?

_____

_____

_____

Understand how powerful you are in God. Greater is He that is in you, than he that is in the world.

Who is "he that is in the world"? What power does he actually have, if any?

_____

When you allow God's power to arise in you, you will do mighty works, you can lay hands on the sick and they shall recover, you have power to cast out demons, you are anointed to speak the Word of God and see miracles, signs, and wonders taking place.

Read Mark 16:17-18.
This is remarkable power! How did Jesus' disciples receive it?

_____

_____

After God's Own Heart

And when He had removed him, He raised up
unto them David to be their king to whom also
He gave testimony, and said, I HAVE FOUND
DAVID the son of Jesse, A MAN AFTER MINE
OWN HEART, which shall fulfil all My will. (Acts
13:22 KJV)

God will always raise up someone to rule and reign over
His Kingdom.
   Who is the King of God's Kingdom?
   (Read Revelation 19:11-16.)

_____

_____

   Oftentimes, people attempt to get their lives straightened
out, because they don't think that God can use someone like
them. God doesn't need permission to do anything. He is
Sovereign. God can do what He wants to, to anyone He wants
to, when and how He wants to.
   Think of some of the people God used in the Bible. Were
their lives all sorted out? Was it their own strength they
operated in, or was it God's strength?

_____

_____

   God is loving and merciful. He gives His people the
opportunity to get it right. The Lord knows the hearts of His

people. He knows when they are feeling guilty, condemned, or convicted. God is looking for a people who will do ALL His will, those who will diligently seek Him wholeheartedly.

Ask Yourself...

How many times has God given you a second chance?

How have you responded to those second chances?

-199-

God Has Entrusted You

But as we were allowed of God to be put in trust with the gospel, even so we speak, not as pleasing men, but God, which trieth our hearts.
(1 Thessalonians 2:4 KJV)

God's Word is a treasure! We carry this treasure around in our hearts. God approves of us when our heart is in right standing with His Word.

Take some time to read all of Psalm 119. Write down all the verses that refer to God's Word or Law as treasure, or as something precious.

_____

_____

_____

_____

_____

God has entrusted us with being a good steward over His Word. We are faithful and responsible messengers of God. Don't worry about how the people will respond to God's Word.

Should we expect others to respond well when we speak the truth to them in love?
(Read Matthew 5:11-12.)

_____

_____

We must deliver His Word with truth and grace.

It is not our responsibility to ensure the Word of God is well-received by others, but it is our responsibility to make sure we present it with as much love and compassion as we can. How can you speak the whole truth with love?

_____

_____

_____

Continue seeking God's approval over man's. The Lord will test our hearts and reward us accordingly.

-200-

Forever

Jesus Christ the same yesterday, and today, and forever. (Hebrews 13:8 KJV)

The Word of God is settled in heaven forever.

Let this truth hover over you. Contemplate what it truly means. Praise and thank God for it, and then write down what you learned.

_____

_____

_____

God's faithfulness will endure throughout all generations. People may change at any time, but JESUS remains the same throughout all eternity.

How often do you change? Can you imagine not changing, ever, for any reason? Can you imagine eternity? Reflect, and record your thoughts.

_____

_____

_____

_____

_____

The Word of God says, "For I am the LORD, I change not." He is Alpha and Omega, the Beginning, and the End, the First and the Last, Who Is, and Who Was, and Who Is to Come, the Almighty; He is God.

Jesus Christ was fully God and fully man. Think about this, and what it means for your relationship with Him. Record your thoughts, and then consult your pastor or Bible teacher to make sure what you wrote lines up with the Word of God.

_____

_____

_____

_____

Before the mountains were brought forth, the Lord formed the earth and the world. He is God, from everlasting to everlasting. His LOVE is forever.

-201-

Blessed All Day Every Day

Blessed shalt thou be in the city, and blessed shalt thou be in the field. Blessed shall be the fruit of thy body, and the fruit of thy ground, and the fruit of thy cattle, the increase of thy kine, and the flocks of thy sheep. Blessed shall be thy basket and thy store. Blessed shalt thou be when thou comest in, and blessed shalt thou be when thou goest out. (Deuteronomy 28:3-6 KJV)

You are blessed all day, every day, whether you acknowledge it or not. You are ALIVE! You are BREATHING! You are blessed because God said so. The BLOOD OF JESUS runs through your veins. You have strength in your body and your organs are functioning properly.

What other blessings has God given you today?

_____

_____

_____

_____

These blessings alone are praiseworthy, but God keeps pouring out His goodness upon you even more. Keep speaking the Word of God. You will encounter the hand of God in your life. Understand that life's situations, circumstances, and troubles doesn't dictate God's love and blessings toward you.

How can you train yourself to see God's blessings in your life, even when things aren't going as well as you'd hoped?

_____

_____

_____

You are Blessed All Day, Every Day! In JESUS' name.

Decree and Declare:

> ➤ *I will see God's blessings in my life every day and thank Him for all of them.*

> ➤ *I am covered by the Blood of Christ, and nothing can come against me.*

-202-

Divine Favor

Remember me, 0 LORD, with the favour that Thou hearest unto Thy people: 0 visit me with Thy salvation. (Psalm 106:4 KJV)

Divine favor is God blessing His people with His supernatural goodness. Who would not like to receive God's divine favor, or who would not want to be treated with God's privileges? The Lord favors His people. He saved us and called us to a holy life, not because of anything we have done, but because of His own purpose and grace.

God's call on our lives should fill us with humility and gratitude, and yet it often does not. Why?

(Read Romans 8:28-32.)

_____

_____

_____

_____

_____

God's love, and His goodness which overwhelms us when divine favor comes, is unfathomable. We can't explain it! We didn't see it coming! But we know it was God favoring us.

What does God's love look like in our lives? How can you recognize it?

_____

_____

_____

_____

Believe in God's Word and rejoice in His prosperity. The Lord will always show favor to His people.

Praise God...

> ➤ *for His love.*
> ➤ *for His divine favor.*
> ➤ *for His supernatural goodness.*
> ➤ *for His Righteousness.*
> ➤ *for His Holy Spirit.*
> ➤ *for our salvation in Christ Jesus!*

-203-

Leap Into Your Destiny

The LORD will perfect that which concerneth me: Thy mercy, O LORD, endureth for ever; forsake not the works of Thine hands. (Psalm 138:8 KJV)

Your destiny is closer than you think. You have stayed in the will of God. You have worked diligently and heeded the voice of the Lord. Now, it's time for you to leap into your destiny. It's time for God's goodness to be poured out upon you.

Ask Yourself...

What have you done to prepare for this moment?

_____

_____

How have you stayed in the will of God?

_____

_____

What is your destiny?

_____

_____

No more stalling, waiting, and delays. You will walk out your purpose, plan, and will for your life. Know that what God has for you *is for you*, and no one can take what belongs to you.

Pray: *Lord, please allow me to fulfill all the purposes You have planned for my life. Now, Lord I turn my own will over unto Your will.*

It's your time to leap into your destiny. Every desire of your heart, every Logos or written Word of God, every Rhema or word spoken over your life, is being manifested.

"Rhema" means "any spoken word." What words have been spoken over you?

_____

_____

-204-

An Expected End

For I know the thoughts that I think toward you, saith the LORD, thoughts of peace, and not of evil, to give you an expected end. (Jeremiah 29:11 KJV)

The Lord holds your future in His Hands. He has a foolproof plan for each of us. His master plan for our lives is filled with favor, blessings, and promises. Continue lying on your face or prostrate and turn your face to the wall in reverencing and seeking the Lord.

Read Isaiah 38:1-8.
Why does King Hezekiah take these postures before the Lord?

_____

_____

Keep His Word and don't stray from it but draw closer to Him. The plans the Lord has for you are greater than anything you could imagine. Your future is bright, successful, and prosperous.

Read Proverbs 23:18 and Revelation 21:1-5.
What do these passages mean for you, right now?

_____

_____

God desires to bless you abundantly, with more than you could have ever believed Him for. Live in expectancy and call forth greater expectations for your life. Receive God's Word; though your beginning was small, yet your latter end will increase abundantly.

Read Job 8:7.
What does this verse mean in context?

_____

_____

Finished Strong

*I have fought a good fight, I have finished my course,
I have kept the faith.* (2 Timothy 4:7 KJV)

Truly the grace of God has covered us and allowed us to master what we could not do in our own strength.

Through much prayer and fasting, God keeps proving Himself to us; we have worked diligently and faithfully.

We have been steadfast and loyal in the things pertaining to the Kingdom of God.

We must remain disciplined and focused on God's purpose, plan, and will for our lives, and we have persevered through difficult situations and circumstances, but God was right there leading, and paving a clear path to our future, opening doors, turning things around in our favor.

With faith and confidence in the Lord, we have great advancement opportunities.

Our Readiness, willingness, and determination served as a greater purpose to do what God has called for us to do and be.

With much practice and endurance, we will reap the benefits of our labor.

My ultimate prayer is that the Lord will grant you His unmerited favor to "FINISH STRONG" in all areas of your life.

Make a plan to finish strong and follow it to the end!

_____

_____

_____

Visit: Kingdom Encounters to receive, (Faith Solutions) from the Word of God, that will change the outcome of your life.

Website: kingdomencountersbooks.com

Email: kingdomencountersbooks@yahoo.com

Author/Writer:
TRUE TESTIMONIES & FOOD FOR THE SOUL

MORE BOOKS ARE ON THE WAY!

LUVERTA H. BOULWARE-RADIO HOST RADIO SHOW-LIFE IS A JOURNEY "EXPECT TO HAVE A KINGDOM ENCOUNTER" VISIT: http://www.WDRBmedia.com LISTEN LIVE 24/7 CLICK ON THE LISTEN LIVE TAB WDRBmedia "the Voice Of The Community" Streaming live through FREE TUNEIN Radio app, Streema, Apple Music, RadioSeed, and more.

Printed in the USA
CPSIA information can be obtained
at www.ICGtesting.com
LVHW020344130524
779982LV00010B/168